ABOUT THE AUTHOR

Karen Jillings is a lecturer in history at Massey University in New Zealand.

SCOTLAND'S
Black Death

The Foul Death of the English

KAREN JILLINGS

TEMPUS

Cover   *ance*
of De*

For Stephen and LS – my family

This edition first published 2007

Tempus Publishing Limited
The Mill, Brimscombe Port,
Stroud, Gloucestershire, GL5 2QG
www.tempus-publishing.com

© Karen Jillings 2003, 2007

British Library Cataloguing in Publication Data.
A catalogue record for this book is available from the British Library.

ISBN 978 07524 3732 3

Typesetting and origination by Tempus Publishing Limited
Printed in Great Britain

CONTENTS

PREFACE

The epidemic known as the Black Death swept across Western Christendom between 1347 and 1351 devastating communities, disrupting the economy and plunging society into unmitigated chaos. By the time it had run its course, at least a third of Europe was dead. Its impact on 'this poor little Scotland, beyond which there is no dwelling place at all' – as the authors of the Declaration of Arbroath described their nation in 1320 – has so far received little attention from historians. In spite of this contemporary view (which was essentially a piece of propaganda that its proponents did not in any case believe) Scotland was, in the fourteenth century, an integral part of Christendom, a country whose apparently peripheral location belied the distinctive contribution it made to European life through the various vibrant commercial, religious, intellectual, diplomatic, cultural and military links it maintained with the continent. Such interaction inevitably led to the transmission of epidemic disease. It was the last of these links, that of military campaigns, that brought the Black Death to Scotland in late 1349. It was spread to Scottish soldiers during a stand-off with English forces in southern Scotland and, from there, was unwittingly carried by these fleeing troops throughout the country. Within a year, at least a quarter of the population had been killed by pestilence.

Such appalling mortality could have had little other than profound practical and psychological consequences, especially as the manifestation of the affliction was both indiscriminate and inexplicable. 'The foul death of the English', as the Scots initially termed the disease, reflected its horrifying nature and its significant deadliness and, in high-lighting its immediately discernible origins, implied the absence of a recognised medical understanding about it. While physicians advanced scientific explanations for the disease, their responses, in common with that of chroniclers and individuals alike, were set against a backdrop of a perva-sive and unquestioned belief in the interpretation of plague as divine retribution for society's sin. Contemporary accounts related that, when the Black Death initially appeared amongst the troops they were fighting, Scottish soldiers 'attributed it to the avenging hand of God ... [believing His] dreadful judgement to have descended upon the English.' Given the timing of the epidemic, it is little wonder that plague should have been viewed in this way, as it struck when the nation's king was in English captivity, in the middle of a century during which the struggle for independence against England dominated political concerns. By the time the Black Death arrived, Scotland's inhabitants had already been significantly weakened by decades of war, famine, political instability and economic misfortune, a result of natural as well as human forces.

While the importance of the Wars of Independence to fourteenth-century Scottish history has rightly been widely recognised by historians, the impact of plague has received little attention. One of the few scholars to note the recognition that the Black Death in Scotland deserves, Audrey-Beth Fitch has commented that 'Scottish scholars… have accepted the analyses of other national historians… without sufficient investigation of peculiarly Scottish conditions.' This may partly be because of the challenging nature of the surviving sources. Chroniclers' accounts are reticent, bureaucratic and economic sources patchy while population statistics are non-existent. Although historians of Scotland have recognised that the Black Death must have been devastating in its impact, they have tended to assume that there is little which can profitably be written about it, even though sufficient clues exist to assess the probable impact of, and responses to, fourteenth-century plague. Similarly, Scotland has been seriously neglected in surveys of the impact of the Black Death throughout Europe, with mentions of it generally relegated to asides in commentary on larger, more 'significant' countries. This has produced apparently contradictory conclusions: Philip Ziegler, in his classic work on the Black Death in Europe, commented on the way in which the country escaped with 'so light a scar' from the disease. On the other hand, in his study of medieval Scotland Alexander Grant noted that the epidemic appears to have been 'the worst disaster suffered by the people of Scotland in recorded history.' This book will examine whether there is any truth in either, or both, of these pronouncements. It is divided into three parts: part one recounts the Black Death in Scotland, putting the epidemic in the context of wider fourteenth-century events. Part two evaluates the effects of the outbreak on Scotland, while part three analyses responses to plague, showing how contemporaries fundamentally turned to their faith as well as medicine to interpret and combat the scourge that so affected them.

In writing this book I have benefited from the help of many people. I should particularly like to record my thanks to Jonathan Reeve for his patience and guidance through the publishing process. I owe a huge debt of gratitude to my doctoral supervisor, William Naphy: without Bill's initial intervention I doubt this book would ever have existed. His constant encouragement and support has long fostered, sustained and developed my interest in historical plague and its effects. Thanks are also due to my parents and sister, each of whom has always been a source of support and inspiration and who helpfully read and commented on earlier drafts. Special thanks must go above all to Stephen Chadwick, who has provided invaluable help and encouragement in every way and, more than anyone else, has been forced to tolerate the spectre of plague in his midst. To all of the above, my heartfelt thanks.

I

The Black Death
in Scotland

n the year 1350 there was, in the kingdom of Scotland, so great a pestilence and plague among men... as, from the beginning of the world even unto modern times, had never been heard of by man, nor is found in books, for the enlightenment of those who come after. For, to such a pitch did that plague wreak its cruel spite, that nearly a third of mankind was thereby made to pay the debt of nature. Moreover, by God's will, this evil led to a strange and unwonted kind of death, insomuch that the flesh of the sick was somehow puffed out and swollen, and they dragged out their earthly life for barely two days. Now this everywhere attacked the meaner sort and common people; – seldom the magnates. Men shrank from it so much that, through fear of contagion, sons, fleeing as from the face of leprosy or an adder, durst not go and see their parents in the throes of death.

John of Fordun's *Chronicle of the Scottish Nation* contains the most detailed account of the Black Death in Scotland. It appeared around 1385, some thirty-five years after both that epidemic and two further (though more localised) outbreaks of plague. His description reveals much that was characteristic of the Black Death throughout Europe: the way in which it killed a huge percentage of the population; the acknowledgement that it came as a result of God's will; the horror and terror it provoked amongst society. Yet there are a few striking anomalies present in Fordun's account that did not seem to have been the case everywhere: the view of the disease as a completely unknown entity; the way in which it was almost exclusively the poor who were killed; the particular way in which the symptoms of the disease were described; the fact that fewer people seemed to have been infected than contemporary estimates recorded elsewhere. In recounting the previously untold story of the Black Death in Scotland, this book will address these and other features of the epidemic to reconstruct a picture not only of the effects of the disease but also the way in which fourteenth-century Scottish society dealt with this horrifying, unprecedented disease.

This study of the Black Death in Scotland appears at a time of renewed interest in the mid-fourteenth century pandemic, as recent findings have questioned the exact clinical nature of the disease that wreaked such literal and psychological devastation amongst Europe's inhabitants, killing a third of them in the course of only a few years. The modern identification of a medieval epidemic is a complex undertaking, hampered, in the absence of incontrovertible bacteriological evidence, by a dependency on contemporary descriptions of symptoms. These, however, are open to interpretation as they differ widely and were often embellished or exaggerated. This is understandable, as we may well imagine the difficulty in writing dispassionately or objectively about something so terrifying and inexplicable.

Contrary to Fordun's protestations, however, outbreaks of plague were not completely unknown to medieval Europe. Assuming the disease to be a completely unknown entity would be doing a great disservice to the inhabitants of four-teenth-century Christendom. Both classical literature and the Bible provided ample evidence not only of the existence of epidemics but also the of terrifying devastation which they caused. From the detailed account of the plague that struck Athens in the fifth century BC, to the deadly plagues inflicted upon the disobedient Egyptians and Philistines by a vengeful God, medieval man understood the horrors of plague and was fully convinced that divine retribution lay behind its arrival. He was also well aware that it could strike closer to home, thanks to the chroniclers who recorded with terrible detail intermittent outbreaks in more recent times.

Indeed, the epidemic of the mid-fourteenth century was not the first plague pandemic to have afflicted Europe, but the second. The First Great Pandemic (as it may be termed) had broken out in AD 540, at a time when the Emperor Justinian sought to reconquer provinces of the western Roman Empire. Known as the Justinian Plague, it broke out in the harbour town of Pelusium and killed millions of inhabitants in the Mediterranean basin and beyond before petering out in AD 590. Though Ireland was said to have been struck by this plague, termed 'blefed' in the Annals of Ulster, Scotland apparently escaped its ravages. While a sub-sequent outbreak in AD 599-600 killed some 15 per cent of the population of Italy and southern France, later outbreaks appear also to have spared those living north of the River Tweed. Before the unification of Scotland under Kenneth MacAlpin in AD 843, the area was inhabited by peoples known as Picts and Scots, the latter group originating in Ulster in the north of Ireland. Contradicting himself some-what, Fordun recorded the First Great Pandemic but noted that its intermittent outbreaks did not reach the Picts or the Scots, although he did note that neither group was entirely free from sin.

While medieval interpretations of the plague had at their core the notion of divine retribution, modern beliefs about the nature and spread of the disease focus on clinical explanations. The disease now known as plague was first identified scientifically in 1894 by Alexandre Yersin, who isolated the bacillus then causing the Third Great Pandemic (1894-99). Originally named *Pasteurella pestis*, it is now more commonly known as *Yersinia pestis* and causes three distinct forms of plague: bubonic (which causes swelling of the lymphatic glands, producing buboes); pneumonic (the bacillus accumulates in the lungs, causing the expulsion of blood and extreme neurological disorders); septicaemic (the bacillus concentrates in the blood stream, producing a rash from thousands of burst capillaries). More recently, a further two strains have been identified: *Yersinia pseudo-tuberculosis* (with symptoms characteristic of tuberculosis) and *Yersinia enterocolita* (which infests the lower digestive tract). There are differences in the manner in which these various manifesta-tions of plague spread, as well as in the degree and speed of fatality. The bubonic form is normally a disease of rats and other rodents, carried from animal to animal by infected fleas. If no rodent host is available, the flea will seek out any warm body, including that of humans. The flea may then regurgitate infected blood into its new host, thereby spreading the bacillus. After an incubation period of between two and eight days, the infected person develops a high fever, giddiness, vomiting and pains in the limbs. This is followed by the swelling of the lymph glands (in the armpit, neck and groin), which will eventually burst. Occasionally, livid crimson-coloured spots may appear on the skin. Death occurs in about 75 per cent of cases and comes after about a week. The most rare form, septicaemic plague, is always fatal. The sufferer becomes infected by a flea bite that expels the bacillus directly into the blood stream. As death occurs so suddenly after infection (within the day), this form of plague is not easily transmitted, though the high concentration of bacillus in the blood makes it possible that human fleas and lice could then spread it. Unlike these two forms, pneumonic plague is not spread by rodent fleas. The bacillus concentrates in the lungs and is spread directly from person to person through coughing, sneezing, or even talking. Within two or three days the patient exhibits neurological disorder and falls into a coma. Death soon follows in over 95 per cent of cases. Being an airborne disease it spreads most effectively in colder, damper climates.

It has long been assumed that bubonic plague was responsible for the Second Great Pandemic, known as the Black Death, spread by the flea of infected rats along trade routes from village to village and country to country. However, recent independent studies conducted in Italy, England and America have cast serious doubt on the assumption that bubonic plague was the causative agent. In April 2002 anthropologists from Pennsylvania State University announced they found it highly unlikely that the disease known to modern medicine as bubonic plague was present to any great extent in the 1340s, in England at least. The method of transmission is the first significant influential factor. Modern medical theories identify bubonic plague as a rodent disease, transmitted from rats to humans through infected fleas. Since bubonic plague cannot be transmitted directly from person to person, an incubation period of two to eight days is irrelevant for enabling the disease to spread. But the thesis of the Black Death being spread by rats is problematic. To begin with, fleas thrive on their preferred rodent hosts and will only move to a human if no rats are available because they have already died. Therefore, it would be expected that an epidemic of bubonic plague would be preceded by a great and noticeable mortality amongst rats. There were no reports of mass rodent deaths recorded in the 1340s, such as those commonly found relating to more recent epidemics known to have been caused by bubonic plague. Moreover, an explanation is required for how rats would physically have been able to spread the infection from place to place. Although bubonic plague has tradition-ally been associated with the black rat, it has increasingly been postulated that the brown rat is in fact the preferred carrier. This species tends to live in houses and has a limited territory, rarely travelling far. Even if the black rat did carry infected fleas, while it might travel a considerable distance in grain sacks or hidden among cloth, it would be unlikely to come into intimate contact with humans. Rat fleas would not stay long on humans anyway. Significantly, while black rats were common in much of Europe, many biologists believe that the arrival of the brown rat occurred only in the eighteenth century.

An analysis of contemporary sources supports the notion that rats did not spread the Black Death. The researchers from Penn State were able to plot the spread of the disease as it moved through the English parish of Lincoln, using the only surviving contemporary bishop's register that listed the date of death. They found that the disease spread more rapidly than had previously been believed and concluded that transmission occurred too fast to be attributable to something first established in the wild rodent population, such as bubonic plague. Researchers at the University of Liverpool concurred with these findings, concluding from various contemporary reports that the epidemic spread at the rate of approximately thirty miles in the space of two or three days. Modern bubonic plague, on the other hand, travels only around a hundred yards a year. If further convincing were needed, it is worth noting that the Black Death spread rapidly along trade routes and navigable rivers with no regard for the geophysical boundaries that would hinder the movement of rodents. The modern culpability of rats as carriers of disease, coupled with the misidentification of the Black Death as bubonic plague has, it seems, led traditionally to erroneous assumptions about the nature and spread of the epidemic.

If the Black Death was not, after all, the insect-borne rodent disease now identified as bubonic plague, then what was it and how was it spread? The anthropologists at Penn

State admitted they could not rule out the possibility of the epidemic being caused by an ancestor of the modern plague bacillus *Yersinia pestis* which has mutated over time. However, they found it more likely that the Black Death was caused by any number of infectious organisms transmitted directly through person-to-person contact. It was spread in the same manner as a modern-day virus, through a person's breath or touch. The theory of a viral cause is supported by the recent discovery of a mutated gene – CCR5 – that is resistant to HIV, the virus which causes AIDS. The first mutation of the gene was calculated as occurring in Europe 650 years ago, coinciding with the Black Death. The process of natural selection left Europe predominately populated by those carrying that gene – currently believed to be between 10 and 18 per cent of people of European descent. The identification of the Black Death as a viral infection explains a number of characteristics of the disease apparent from contemporary accounts – and implies certain others. It was able to spread rapidly from person to person, unhindered by geophysical boundaries. It killed quickly, which implies that its transmission was faster and more effective in areas of dense population. The precise identification of the nature of the Black Death is rather harder to establish and hence remains a matter for debate. Contemporary accounts of symptoms clearly hold the key, but they are equally open to interpretation. The classic account of symptoms is provided in the *Decameron*, by the Italian writer Giovanni Boccaccio:

> ...in men and women alike [the disease] first betrayed
> itself by the emergence of certain tumours in the
> groin or the armpits, some of which grew as large as
> a common apple, others as an egg, some more, some
> less, which the common folk called *gavocciolo*. From the
> two said parts of the body this deadly *gavocciolo* soon
> began to propagate and spread itself in all directions
> indifferently; after which the form of the malady began
> to change, black spots or livid making their appearance
> in many cases on the arm or the thigh or elsewhere,
> now few and large, now minute and numerous. And as
> the *gavocciolo* had been and still were an infallible token
> of approaching death, such also were these spots on
> whomsoever they shewed themselves...

The most common descriptions record swellings, termed
buboes, which have traditionally led to its identification as
bubonic plague. However, researchers at the University of
Liverpool have pointed out that swellings are symptomatic of
numerous diseases. Other symptoms mentioned for the Black
Death, such as fever, chills and vomiting blood, accord more
with viral diseases such as Spanish influenza, West Nile virus
and ebola. This last disease has caused particular concern since
its discovery in 1976 in Zaire. Transmitted most commonly
through contact with the bodily fluids of infected patients, it
is extremely contagious and its symptoms are agonising. It is
a hemorrhagic fever that strikes fast, bringing the victim out
in a visible swollen rash caused by the blood vessels bursting
underneath the skin. As well as developing a fever and sore
throat, sufferers often spit blood and the internal organs also

collapse and liquidise, producing a fetid black liquid. Death occurs in 50–90 per cent of clinically ill cases.

Establishing which disease may have been present in the epidemic that reached Scotland in late 1349 is complicated by there being only a few accounts that record symptoms. As the most contemporaneous and detailed description, Fordun is perhaps also the most credible. He described how 'this evil led to a strange and unwonted kind of death, insomuch that the flesh of the sick was somehow puffed out and swollen, and they dragged out their earthly life for barely two days.' The anonymous author of *The Book of Pluscarden*, written only slightly later, noted that victims 'were attacked with inflammation and lingered barely four and twenty hours.' These descriptions are noteworthy as they provide an indication not only of symptoms but also of the speed with which victims were killed. Both allude to the appearance of swellings covering a substantial part of the body and, significantly, both provide a strong indication that sufferers died within a short space of time, from one to three days. This last point alone would seem to discount bubonic plague, which prolongs sufferers' agony for about a week before either death or recovery. Indeed, the quick deaths accord more with pneumonic plague, which usually kills within two days. The presence of pneumonic plague in Scotland has been considered credible by historians, not only because it kills quickly but also because this strain of the disease favours colder climates. It tends to be more prevalent during the winter months: the Black Death, so far as it can be dated, first reached Scotland in the winter of 1349 (hence Fordun's assertion that it was widespread in 1350). Molecular biologists at a university in

Marseilles recorded in 1998 that they had discovered the plague bacillus *Yersinia pestis* in remains dating from 1348, as well as 1590 and 1722. It may be the case, therefore, that what is now considered plague at least played a role in the Black Death pandemic and that it was the pneumonic form that hit Scotland, perhaps with a secondary septicaemic strain. It is interesting that there was no mention of spots or 'tokens' on the body, nor of other symptoms commonly reported elsewhere, such as severe headaches and the vomiting of blood. This would seem to indicate that several different strains of the disease were present, or at least that they manifested themselves differently depending on external factors such as climate. We must also bear in mind that some deaths may have been due to other, secondary, infections. Whatever its symptoms, if recent research is correct then the Black Death may have been due to a viral infection which travelled rapidly amongst people in close proximity. This would fit in with the chroniclers' comments on the way in which the epidemic reached Scotland, it reportedly having been spread from English soldiers fighting Scottish forces in the Borders. The English chronicler Henry Knighton recorded its arrival:

> The Scots, hearing of the cruel plague amongst the English, attributed it to the avenging hand of God, and took it up as an oath, as a common report came to English ears, and when they wished to swear they would say 'By the filthy death of England' (or in English: 'Be the foul dethe of Engelond'). And thus the Scots, believing God's dreadful judgement to have descended

upon the English, gathered in the forest of Selkirk ready
to over run [sic] the whole kingdom of England. And
a fierce pestilence arose, and blew a sudden and mon-
strous death upon the Scots, and some 5,000 of them
died in a short time, and the rest of them, some fit and
some enfeebled, prepared to make their way home, but
the English pursued them and fell upon them, and slew
a great many of them.

This account provides further testimony that pneumonic
plague may have played a role. This form of plague is transmitted from person to person without the need for an inter-
mediary and is over 95 per cent fatal within a couple of days.
This accords with Knighton's assertion that the plague spread
quickly among the Scots and killed many within a short
space of time. The transmission of the disease during the
course of fighting would also suggest that it was passed by
person-to-person contact rather than by infected rodent fleas.
Moreover, the Scottish Urban Archaeological Trust has found
absolutely no conclusive evidence for the presence of black
rats at medieval Scottish sites. Neither were rats apparently
present in Iceland when that country was struck by plague.
The precise death rate cannot easily be established and we
may wonder how many 'the rest of them' actually numbered.
Knighton's account is valuable as it is the only one to give
so much as an approximate figure for the number of Scots
killed when plague first struck. Of course, his figures are no
more credible than those of, for example, the chronicler of
Meaux Abbey who reported a force of 90,000 Scots at the
siege of Berwick in 1333 and, ultimately, it must be con-

cluded that, in postulating a figure of 5,000, what Knighton really meant was that a great number had died. In citing such a high figure the chronicler at least implied the important point that contemporaries believed plague to have struck viciously. Even taking into account the assumption that a small proportion would have escaped infection altogether (perhaps the 'fit' people to whom Knighton refers), then, in the absence of statistical evidence for garrison sizes, we might plausibly conclude that a fatality even of half the quoted amount would have represented a significant percentage of those who were infected. Those who survived at all (both the 'fit' and 'enfeebled') perhaps numbered no more than 10 per cent. However small the percentage, some were spared and the dispersal of these survivors was sufficient to ensure that the Black Death did not remain confined to the southern part of Scotland.

Exactly how far it did manage to spread and how much of the Scottish population was consequently killed by it, is difficult to establish. No local records survive to tell us about the localised impact, so we must turn instead to the chroniclers. None mentions the outbreak's presence in any specific detail. No devastation of a particular area was recorded outside the plague's initial arrival in the south of the country. Indeed, accounts are extremely vague. Fordun commented that the plague was present 'in the kingdom of Scotland', but did not elaborate. Andrew of Wyntoun, writing only slightly later, applied a similarly blanket description of the plague's course:

> *In Scotland, the fyrst Pestilens*
> *Begouth, off sa gret wyolens,*

That it was sayd, off lywand men
The thyrd part it dystroyid then
Efftyr that in till Scotland
A yhere or more it was wedand
Before that tyme was nevyr sene
A pestilens in oure land sa kene:
Bathe men and barnys and women
It sparryed noucht for to kille them.

A metrical version of Hector Boece's chronicle, written in the 1540s, similarly recorded that 'sic pestilence rang ouir all Scotland.' If we assume that the spread of pestilence was dependent upon the close proximity of people, it follows that the denser the spread of population throughout the country then the greater the likelihood of infection. Although the settlement distribution throughout fourteenth-century Scotland was rather more even than is the case today, the country was sparsely populated. Circumstantial evidence indicates that the nation shared in the huge population explosion that occurred throughout Europe during the twelfth and thirteenth centuries and Alexander Grant's reasons for calculating a total population figure of around a million for the early fourteenth century are extremely plausible. A million was the approximate figure in 1707 and, given that agricultural production had changed little, it is clear that medieval Scotland could have supported such a population too. This figure is about a sixth of that of England, a ratio which also ties in with the countries' comparative wealth in the late thirteenth century, most notably in terms of money supplies.

The fairly even distribution of those million Scots was partly due to the absence of a dichotomy between urban and rural living caused by the relative lack of large urban areas. About 90 per cent of the population lived in scattered rural communities known as touns, whose distribution was based on the pastoral system that characterised the country's agriculture. The tenants of these touns paid rent (either in cash or in kind) to their nearest landlord, whose total amount of land varied considerably, from huge earldoms and lordships down to small estates comprising only a couple of touns. The average size was between ten and twenty touns and was known either as a shire, a thanage, or (most commonly by around 1300) a barony. Geological factors determined where people lived and the Highlands and western isles were the least hospitable areas of the country, as well as being the least agriculturally viable. However, this by no means prevented people living there and settlements were as common in the Highlands as in the south of the country. Rather than a Highland/Lowland divide, in fourteenth-century Scotland there was instead a division north and south of the River Forth. Much of the southern part of the country – present-day Lothian and the Borders – was comprised of royal forests and was extremely sparsely populated. Most of the country's inhabitants lived north of the river, with an average density of eleven people per square kilometre, making it generally far less densely populated than most other parts of Europe. However, Scotland's mountainous areas must have entailed regional differences, meaning that in more hospitable parts of the country the density of people would have been more akin to that found in England, France and the Low Countries, each of which had a density of thirty-five to forty per square kilometre.

While 90 per cent of the population lived in scattered rural communities, the remaining 90,000 lived in urban communities known as burghs, established either by the Crown (royal burghs) or major landowners (ecclesiastical burghs and burghs of barony). It is uncertain precisely when the earliest of these was officially established: one twelfth-century Moroccan commentator described Scotland as being 'uninhabited [with] neither town nor village.' This was not exactly accurate, though his comment is noteworthy for highlighting the relative lack of towns. The earliest documentary evidence for the establishment of burghs dates from the first half of the twelfth century, though this should not be taken to mean they did not exist prior to this time. Settlements were established from an early period wherever there were the geophysical resources, such as rivers, to ensure their viability. Dunfermline, Aberdeen and St Andrews are just three examples of burghs that existed before formal receipt of their legal rights. By 1306 there were thirty-eight royal burghs and eighteen non-royal ones. Although firm statistics for individual towns are non-existent, it is clear that none maintained a particularly substantial population. In the thirteenth century, Berwick was the wealthiest town in Scotland and in 1302 it maintained an estimated population of around 1,500. This was slightly larger than the vast majority of burghs, each of which numbered no more than 1,000 while only the four 'great towns of Scotland' – Aberdeen, Edinburgh, Perth and Dundee, according to a commentator from Bruges in 1348 – held more than 2,000. Even by the sixteenth century,

Aberdeen had a population of only around 5,000 and the largest city (and Scotland's capital), Edinburgh, contained no more than 12,500 people in 1560. While the fourteenth-century French chronicler Jean Froissart described Edinburgh as 'the Paris of Scotland', this can be taken more as a comment on that burgh's already emerging dominance, rather than an exact comparison. In general, Scottish towns were smaller than their European counterparts, though huge cities such as London or Paris were exceptional.

The identification of the Black Death as a disease communicable without the intervention of rodents is of equal, if not more, significance in assessing its ability to spread through towns as well as the countryside. The typical conditions in medieval towns are well known: images abound of filthy, dung-laden streets, of animals and people living together in close proximity, with little or no regard paid to issues of hygiene or cleanliness. Such conditions provide ideal breeding grounds for the spread of infected rats and their fleas, which hop from rodent to human with ease, transmitting bubonic plague with devastating ferocity. Certainly the brown rat – the favoured carrier over the black rat – chose to settle in dwellings, nesting and breeding within the warm confines of the typical medieval house. If, instead, we choose to eliminate rodents from any discussion of the Black Death, we must ask ourselves if such conditions were equally conducive to allow the spread of a viral disease and whether, indeed, they were typical of burgh dwellings. The simple answer is 'yes' on both counts.

Though no burgh numbered more than a few thousand, the majority of their inhabitants nevertheless lived in extremely close proximity. Burgh boundaries were dictated by geophysical factors and often limited by the presence of rugged terrain or swampy marshland. Houses tended to be crowded together along the streets, with long plots of land stretching behind (known as backlands or rigs), an indication of the desire to maximise the space available. Where land availability permitted, the backlands would be separated by a common close: otherwise houses would run together along a rig to create a terrace with shared walls. They were usually constructed from a timber frame surrounded by wattle walls, made from thin, interwoven branches and clad with mud, dung, peat or turf. Roofs were typically made from heather, thatch or straw. Not surprisingly, excavations have shown that destruction by fire was very common. Dwellings seldom lasted longer than twenty years and rebuilding every few years was far from unheard of. At least rebuilding was fairly easily achieved: the French chronicler Jean Froissart (who visited Scotland in the 1360s) rather snootily remarked that, after Lothian was ravaged by the English in 1385, 'the people of the country made light of it, saying that with six or eight stakes they could soon have new houses.'

It takes little effort to imagine the dark, crowded and smelly conditions in which typical inhabitants lived. Windows were small and animals shared the living space, confined to a byre end with a drained stony floor. Cooking was frequently done inside on a hearth, which also provided the source of warmth. Furniture was wooden and lighting afforded by candles made with sheep's fat or ceramic lamps fuelled with linseed oil. Most of these structures had internal latrines, comprised of timber-framed pits. However, not every resident lived in dwellings like these: status afforded larger, sturdier houses with separate rooms and an external latrine chamber. The very wealthiest citizens possessed stone houses such as one dating from the late fourteenth century excavated in Edinburgh, with a brightly coloured tiled floor and a sophisticated chute for the disposal of rubbish. As this example proves, it should not be assumed that fourteenth-century burgh dwellers were 'backward', with no regard for sanitation and no skills to implement it. Efforts could be made to facilitate drainage, as proven by excavations in Perth uncovering a wooden sluice gate dating from around 1200. It is true that hygiene was not given much consideration, but in an age before the recognition (however tenuous) of a link between dirt and disease, there was simply no need to be unduly concerned with cleanliness. Unbeknownst to contemporaries, therefore, conditions inside the typical burgh dwelling would easily have permitted infection to pass from person to person. The communication of disease through coughing, sneezing or even talking would have been perfectly possible, facilitated by a general scant regard for sanitation.

Both within and outwith individual burghs, the distribution and density of Scotland's fourteenth-century population are significant for assessing the ease with which a human-to-human communicable disease might have spread. Inhabitants were distributed sparsely throughout the country, with a concentration (such as it was) north of the Forth/Clyde line. With 90 per cent of people living in the countryside there was not a sharp distinction between rural and urban areas. It is probable that, throughout Europe as a whole, the Black Death affected those living in rural areas to a far greater degree than did subsequent epidemics. Quite apart from being further proof that rodent-borne bubonic plague was not responsible, this implies that the Scottish population may have been more susceptible because of its sparsely scattered distribution. However, it could have been the case that many areas of the country practically escaped altogether. Both Fordun and the *Pluscarden* author emphasise that the lower classes were worst hit in the outbreak, 'seldom the magnates.' This may partly have been because, while conditions in rural dwellings were similar to those in burgh houses, much of the nobility lived in comparative – and more isolated – luxury. Castles and, more commonly, tower houses were often built at least partly of stone, strategically placed on cliffs and hills, beside or in lochs, or accessible only via a drawbridge over an encircling moat. Rooms were larger and better ventilated, with more sophisticated sanitation systems and separate dining and sleeping facilities. The nobility may also have managed to escape infection by following physicians' advice and taking flight to these fortified residences. Craigmillar Castle, outside Edinburgh, seems to be one such example where nobles apparently sought refuge during later outbreaks. They certainly had the means to do so, leaving 'the meaner sort and common people' to face plague alone. The chroniclers may have been correct, as the numbers of magnates, though small, remained fairly static after the Black Death (and could even have increased): forty-eight were named in the Declaration of Arbroath (1320) and fifty-six were listed as performing personal homage at Robert II's coronation in 1371. To establish whether flight and living condi-

*Flight of the townspeople: when plague broke out physicians recommended
fleeing from the source of infection, a course of action often taken by many
wealthier members of society including David II*

tions might indeed have enabled them to avoid infection, we
must again return to the likely nature of the Black Death.
Whatever modern identification we may choose to give it,
one thing that is clear is that it killed its victims quickly: in
Fordun's opinion, two or three days; the author of the *Book
of Pluscarden* talks about twenty-four hours. This may have
prevented the disease travelling far, especially in the event of
a particularly lethal strain, as it is likely that sufferers tended
to die too quickly. Perhaps the psychological effects should
not be forgotten either: if Fordun was correct in noting that
the fear of contagion prevented people from visiting their
infected loved ones, then in some cases this may inadvertently
have helped further to prevent the spread of plague.

However, the hypotheses should not be stretched too far.
Such factors would not have impeded it altogether and an
incubation period of even a day or two was probably sufficient to enable it to be carried to the next town. We do
not know precisely to what extent the Black Death reached
every corner of the country, though it is to be expected that

the impact would have been worse in those areas where geophysical features made for denser habitation. Subsequent fourteenth-century outbreaks probably followed the same pattern, though to what extent is difficult to gauge. It may have been the case that the next epidemic after the Black Death – that of 1361-62 – was of a more deadly and therefore more localised form. Bower recorded that 'it spread its strength and virulence as much among nobles and magnates as among common people and other persons of intermediate rank... it took its course in the same way... as before.' As a result David II,

> accompanied by many of the more wealthy and more noble men of the kingdom, withdrew to the northern parts of the same kindom, partly because of the horrible sights and sounds of the multitude of ill and dead, partly because of fear and alarm at that pestilence which was then spreading in the southern parts of that kingdom, and which he planned to escape in good health.

This account implies that infection was confined to the south of the country. Perhaps in that instance the nature of the disease was such that victims were killed too quickly to spread infection far at all, thus ensuring that the north may not have been affected. Since more people lived in that half of the country, mortality in the second outbreak was probably lower than the Black Death. Certainly both the second outbreak and subsequent fourteenth-century ones (1379-80 and, possibly, 1392) were barely accorded a mention by chroniclers. Bower's assertion that a third of the country again perished during the epidemic of 1380 is rather incredible given that he only mentions the event in one sentence. In 1401 a further outbreak is noted with the same nonchalance. It was termed the 'fourth mortality' by Fordun, another indication that Scotland escaped at least one of the epidemics to have hit England, as an outbreak there in 1390 was termed the 'fifth pest' by one chronicler. It may be the case that Scotland did not suffer greatly from subsequent outbreaks, perhaps for similar factors as those which governed its comparative escape from the Black Death. Nevertheless, in cumulative terms they were significant, for any inordinate death rate (even if comparatively small) would have hindered the population's ability to recover its normal levels, especially as the second outbreak occurred only a decade after the Black Death. The cumulative effect would also have had an impact on factors other than the demographic situation: post Black Death economic statistics date only from 1372, by which time the second outbreak had already taken its toll.

Diet was another factor in warding off disease and facilitating recovery if infection was not severe. An emphasis on pastoral farming, dictated by the country's geophysical features, was reflected in the relatively healthy diet that fourteenth-century Scots enjoyed, a fact which attracted comment from foreign observers. The typical diet was based on oatmeal (in porridge and oatcakes) and bere, a form of barley (in ale and broth), supplemented by milk and cheese. An Italian commentator from the thirteenth century cited milk as Scotland's chief product, an observation echoed by a contemporary English chronicler who noted that the Scots' diet consisted mainly of milk, butter, cheese and meat. Aside from beef, lamb, chicken, rabbit and pigeon, fish was also consumed, apparently in remarkable quantities. In the thirteenth century the English monk Ranulph Higden noted that the Scots 'fedde more with flesche, fisches, white meat and with fruits', a diet which changed little over the following centuries. These comments are attested to by archaeological evidence, with oats, barley and rye being the most common grains discovered. Kale, a form of cabbage, was the most frequently eaten vegetable, with peas and beans also consumed. Wild fruit and nuts were eaten on a seasonal basis, including cherries, apples, brambles, raspberries and hazelnuts. Fragments of grapes, figs and walnuts, which originated in the eastern Mediterranean and Middle East, have also been found, as well as various imported spices which were used to flavour dishes (and to hide the taste of rancid meat). These, however, would only have been the luxury of the wealthiest citizens.

The resilience of the population was also influenced by its general health. For fourteenth-century Scots life was hard and short. Diseases such as what we can now identify as tuberculosis were rife, as was infant mortality. The best indications of lifestyle are provided by the many instances of damage to bones caused by repeated exertions. Vertical stress on the body was common, caused by lifting heavy weights, and is evident in both men and women. Excavations from Aberdeen and Linlithgow provide some indication of life expectancy. Of the 207 individuals found at the latter site, 58 per cent died before the age of eighteen, while in Aberdeen this figure was 33 per cent. Half of all those died before they reached their sixth birthday. Fewer than 25 per cent of the adults reached middle age and very few achieved old age. Statistics elsewhere indicate that such life expectancy was comparatively low: out of 216 skeletons examined from a medieval cemetery in Cork, 24 per cent died before their early twenties, with 48 per cent of these dying between the ages of sixteen and twenty. In York 27 per cent of the population died by the age of fourteen while 56 per cent of women and 36 per cent of men died before their mid-thirties. The Aberdeen skeletons correspond with this: unlike today, on average men lived longer than women.

The evidence so far suggests that Scotland was, in quantative terms at least, not hit as hard by the Black Death as other areas of Europe. Perhaps the most appalling fact about the pandemic, and the one which has ensured its enduring fascination, is the sheer mortality it caused. In its wake, Pope Clement VI (1291-1352) estimated that 23,840,000 people had been killed throughout Christendom as a whole, out of a total population of 75 million – in other words, 31 per cent. What his advisors really meant to impart by this was that a huge number of people had died: their calculations were probably fairly near the mark, as historians are in general agreement that around a third of Europe perished from the disease. It has recently been calculated that Europe's population fell from 80 million to 30 million in the pandemic's immediate aftermath. There were, of course, extreme variations in local death rates: the Italian city of Milan is noticeable for being comparatively unaffected though, to this day, the reasons cannot satisfactorily be explained. Recent calculations for other cities are more sobering: Venice lost as much as 60 per cent of its people and almost three quarters of Bremen's residents died.

More often than not contemporaries reported huge fatalities and often spoke of whole villages being wiped out. With regard to England, Knighton recorded that:

> after the plague many buildings, both large and small, in all the cities, boroughs, and townships, decayed and were utterly razed to the ground for want of occupants, and similarly many villages and hamlets were deserted, with not a house left in them, for all who had lived there were dead, and it is likely that many of those villages will never be inhabited again.

Similarly, a monk from Tynemouth recorded that 'very many country towns and quarters of innumerable cities are left altogether without inhabitants.' Such accounts were understandably prone to exaggeration, probably a reflection of their authors' sheer horror at having to witness such agonising death on an unprecedented scale. This in itself is instructive. The most striking thing about the accounts of the Black Death by Scottish chroniclers is the reiterated statement that a third of the population died in the outbreak (in fact, Fordun, the most detailed chronicler, places the figure at 'nearly a third'). This is remarkably conservative in comparison with their counterparts elsewhere, particularly if we take into account medieval chroniclers' tendency to exaggerate. Admittedly no local accounts exist to provide any indication of death tolls for individual towns or areas. Indeed, it is impossible to trace the actual course of the Black Death throughout Scotland, or to comment with any degree of certainty on the likely impact of plague on particular areas.

However, there is little reason to discount the notion that Scotland was hit to almost the same extent as the European average. A death toll of a third seems plausible, given the longer-term picture. It has been estimated that, in line with England, the population did not reach pre-plague levels again until well into the sixteenth century. While immediate population losses from the Black Death might have been replaced, the reoccurrence of plague later in the fourteenth century and beyond accentuated plague's initial impact and its effect in keeping the population low for many years. However, the overall loss after a century might have been relatively small. A poem entitled 'The Harp', probably written in the 1450s,

Death triumphant: The Black Death killed about a third of Scotland's inhabitants. With such catastrophic mortality it is little wonder that contemporaries felt the spectre of Death in their midst much more acutely than ever before

described Scotland as 'fertile of folk, with grete scantness of fude.' Several famines had occurred from the 1420s onwards and the consequent shortage of produce may have accentuated the impression that the population was expanding faster than was actually the case.

Contemporary accounts provide further indications that, in losing around a third of its population, Scotland escaped relatively unscathed from the Black Death compared with the rest of Europe. Significantly, Scottish chroniclers are frustratingly reticent. Compare Fordun's straightforward account, which mentions only the barest facts regarding the symptoms of plague and reactions to victims, with Agnolo di Tura's colourful and heart-rending description of the outbreak in Siena:

> Father abandoned child, wife, husband; one brother, another, for this illness seemed to strike through the breath and the sight. And so they died. And no-one could be found to bury the dead for money or for friendship… And in many places in Siena great pits were dug and piled deep with huge heaps of the dead… And I, Agnolo di Tura, called the Fat, buried my five children with my own hands, and so did many others likewise. And there were also many dead throughout the city who were so sparsely covered with earth that the dogs dragged them forth and devoured their bodies.

This cannot be attributable merely to Italian passion or to the possibility that Fordun was able to write dispassionately because he suffered no personal loss. The reticence of all Scottish chroniclers suggests instead that Scotland was simply not affected on so bad a scale. Historians have often pointed out that chroniclers devoted just as much attention to an outbreak of fowl pest which had decimated the nation's poultry in 1347. Equally striking is the lack of comment on the effects of the plague. There was nothing akin to the detailed reports of other chroniclers of the devastation the epidemic wrought. Most chroniclers described the turmoil into which society was plunged: the shortage of priests and labourers, the fall in prices and rents, the scramble to receive absolution in the face of death. These effects were common across Europe. None of this was recorded with regard to Scotland. This is not to imply that no such effects were apparent to any extent, for they are discernible from other sources. But it is surely significant that Scottish chroniclers did not see fit to accord them so much as a mention. It is plausible to conclude with some certainty that Scotland was less badly affected by the Black Death than other areas of Western Europe. Non-native commentators may likewise have believed that Scotland escaped lightly, or even altogether. Take the summary of the course of the epidemic recorded by one English monk:

> In the year of our Lord 1348, and in the month of August, there began the deadly pestilence in England which three years previously had commenced in India, and then had spread through all Asia and Africa, and coming into Europe had depopulated Greece, Italy, Provence, Burgundy, Spain, Aquitaine, Ireland, France, with its subject provinces, and at length England and Wales...

It is interesting that a chronicler from a neighbouring country should have omitted Scotland from his account, especially given his inclusion of Ireland and Wales. Contemporary reports from both countries attest to the fact that they were badly affected by plague. The Welsh poet Jeuan Gethin noted in the spring of 1349 that 'we see death coming into our midst like black smoke, a plague which cuts off the young, a rootless phantom which has no mercy for fair countenance.' The Irish friar John Clyn from Kilkenny was similarly horror-struck by the suffering and mortality he witnessed, declaring that:

> in case things which should be remembered perish with time and vanish from the memory of those who are to come after us, I, seeing so many evils and the whole world, as it were, placed within the grasp of the evil one, being myself as if among the dead, waiting for death to visit me, have put into writing truthfully all the things that I have heard.

Even allowing for a degree of hyberbole on the part of these and other commentators, it seems remarkable that Scottish chroniclers did not wax lyrical in their own accounts of the Black Death. If Fordun was able to look back with such comparative calm on the events of thirty years before, it is plausible that Scotland escaped relatively lightly from the outbreak (and subsequent bouts). Indeed, in his classic study of the Black Death in Europe, Philip Ziegler considered it unsurprising that the outbreak 'left so light a scar' on

'Gebeyn aller menschen', *a cemetery*

Scotland. Nevertheless, the death of a third, a quarter or even a fifth of the population must have caused considerable economic disruption, not to mention a serious psychological effect on those who were left. On a worldwide scale, a 33 per cent death rate would be equivalent to the entire population of India and China dying without a sole survivor in five years – a mind-boggling amount. While our modern-day theorising about the clinical nature of the epidemic enables us to speculate about the probable extent of the disease, ultimately it is of no relevance. To Scots living in the time of the Black

Death, the knowledge that statistically they escaped relatively lightly would have been of absolutely no comfort. The impact of the epidemic on individuals would have been felt as keenly as if a larger percentage of their countrymen had died. Indeed, aside from Alexander Grant's pronouncement that the epidemic appears to have been 'the worst disaster suffered by the people of Scotland in recorded history', David Ditchburn has described it as 'arguably the single most traumatic event in the medieval Scottish experience.' The way in which Scottish society would have responded to such a traumatic experience and the factors which made it so, are discussed in the remaining chapters.

2

The Effects of the
Black Death in Scotland

he Black Death has traditionally been regarded as marking a watershed in the history of Western Europe. Early scholars believed it heralded an irrevocable and monumental change both in social structure and consciousness. It has variously been credited with marking the end of the Middle Ages, initiating the Renaissance and instigating the decline of Catholicism and the subsequent onset of the Reformation. It might almost be said that, for those of this opinion, had the Black Death not occurred, then the course of European history would have been significantly different. More recently, others have sought to revise this view and play down the impact of the pandemic. They hold that the rot had already set in; that Europe was already experiencing economic and demographic decline before the mid-fourteenth century. Rather than marking an epoch in Western European history, therefore, the Black Death has been judged in this view merely to have accentuated existing trends. Whichever proposition one chooses to believe, the argument demonstrates the importance of placing the pandemic in context. The scale of mortality itself ensured the Black Death's notoriety: it may well be imagined that, whatever the state of society at the outset of plague's arrival, a death rate of a third over the course of four years entailed catastrophic results. As the population fell so did productivity, leading to a downturn in trade and a rise in prices. Peasants became far better off, especially as the scarcity of ready labour enabled the workforce to demand higher wages. We must ask ourselves to what extent these effects were apparent in Scotland and whether plague instigated or exacerbated profound change.

In order to assess the effects of the Black Death, it is necessary to appreciate the conditions under which it broke out. Historians are in general agreement that, during the two centuries preceding the Black Death, Europe as a whole had enjoyed a period of massive economic growth. Scotland certainly was no exception. The evidence suggests that thirteenth-century Scotland's economy was basically booming. In line with general European developments, there was an increase in the money supply, despite a concurrent rise in the population. This entailed a greater competition for land and consequent higher rents. Despite these pressures, peasants who farmed sheep were still able to benefit from the buoyant wool sales that continued throughout the century. The main benefactors from a prosperous economy were the landed classes who could afford to purchase lands further afield. By the early fourteenth century, practically every Scottish earl, many lesser nobles and at least eight monasteries owned land in England and/or Ireland, from which they almost certainly profited.

However, the thirteenth-century economy was not without its problems: episodes of sheep scab in 1268 and 1272, for example, would have been disastrous for an economy so heavily reliant on those animals. The reign of Alexander III (1249-86), whose death in 1286 plunged Scotland into the milieu of uncertainty over royal succession and led to the onset of the Wars of Independence, was described by one historian as perhaps not quite a golden age of prosperity, but very definitely a silver one. This seems an appropriate adage to apply to thirteenth-century Europe as a whole.

By the end of the thirteenth century, Scotland was embroiled in a struggle for national independence against England that would dominate governmental concerns throughout the fourteenth century and beyond. The death of Alexander and subsequently that of his granddaughter Margaret entailed a 'competition' for the Scottish throne known as the 'Great Cause', which was presided over by the formidable English king Edward I. The Anglo-Scottish conflict broke out in 1296, with the forced abdication, imprisonment and later exile of Scotland's king, John Balliol, by the English. The guardians who governed Scotland thereafter refused to recognise Balliol's abdication and directed the 'community of the realm' – representing the whole of Scottish society – in a subsequent struggle for his reinstatement. With the collapse of the unified front they tried to present, the nation was forced to submit to the English in 1304. This acquiescence was to be short-lived: a recognition of the need for strong leadership resulted in the emergence of Robert Bruce who usurped the throne and crowned himself king in 1306. In the course of his revolt he murdered his main rival, John Comyn, thus starting a civil war which was fought out concurrently with the continuing Anglo-Scottish hostilities. In this arena Bruce was successful, both militarily – with the Scots' famous victory at Bannockburn in 1314 – and diplomatically, with Scotland's independence formally acknowledged with the Treaty of Edinburgh in 1328. While Bruce's successes in the latter conflict proved his greatest achievement, the Bruce-Balliol rivalry divided Scotland's nobility and was not resolved until the late 1340s.

Neither was the conflict with England. The Treaty of Edinburgh brought only a temporary cessation of hostilities and, with Bruce's death the following year, it was not long before Scotland was mourning more than the loss of one of its greatest kings. He had died leaving a five-year-old son, David, and those who ruled the kingdom in his minority proved inadequate. The lack of effective leadership laid Scotland open to attack by both disgruntled Scottish nobles and the English, ruled since 1327 by Edward III. With the young king David II sent to France for safety, open hostilities were resumed with a series of onslaughts by both sides carried out throughout the 1330s. The Scots successfully repelled periodic attack and were able to bring David II back in 1341 but the wars had taken their toll on the country. Many nobles had been killed, the countryside had been pillaged and wasted by scorched-earth tactics, much expenditure had gone into the war effort and military success was due as much to individual efforts as to those of a nation unified in the face of enemy aggression.

Moreover, David II's return did not mean the end of the struggle with England. Edward III still refused to renounce his claim to Scotland and continued to repudiate the terms of the Treaty of Edinburgh. David sought to quash English encroachment by military force and launched a series of raids on northern England in 1342, 1345 and 1346. Ostensibly, he was aided in this by the concurrent English conflicts with France which had led to open warfare in 1337 with the outbreak of the Hundred Years' War. In 1346 the English were engaged in conflict with the French at the siege of Calais and David saw the Scots' chance to attack. It was also an opportunity to fulfil the terms of the Treaty of Corbeil that Scotland and France, uniting in the face of a common enemy, had signed in 1326, promising mutual assistance in the event of English encroachment. David, therefore, gathered a huge army and launched an invasion in October 1346, with disastrous results. In the event, the English were fully prepared for the attack and defeated the Scots at Neville's Cross, outside Durham. Many Scottish nobles were killed or captured as a result and David himself was taken prisoner. While this was clearly a setback, in practical terms it was not especially significant. This is evidenced by Edward III being forced to reduce his demands in return for the king's release, one of which was a ransom of £40,000. His other demands – including overlordship and succession by an English king if David died childless – were eventually dispensed with altogether in favour of a straightforward ransom of 100,000 merks (£66,667). The Scots' acceptance of this was made formal with the Treaty of Berwick in 1357, though in practice they were neither willing nor able to pay it.

In early fourteenth-century Scotland the war against England and the accompanying Scottish civil war caused the most significant disruption to society. The wars took their toll and were arguably the biggest instigator of fourteenth-century socio-economic change aside from the Black Death. Inevitably, war produces casualties other than of those engaged in actual combat. Even if the actual cost in terms of human

lives was relatively small, the destruction of crops and dwellings and the disruption caused to rural life must not only have
had a significant financial impact, but also have reduced agricultural production. Petitions to Edward I for compensation as
a result of the fighting provide testimony to the financial losses
incurred. In the aftermath of the siege of Berwick (1333), those
from a nearby church complained that 'during the siege their
church and houses were struck down by siege-engines so that
they had no place of refuge.' Even though the master of the
house had used up all his resources paying for its repair, 'the
building is [now] so weak that it cannot withstand the winter
without rotting forever.' Individuals also suffered heavy losses.
Robert de Tughale lamented that his houses in Northumberland 'have been burnt and destroyed by the Scots… and
standing grain, namely 80 acres of wheat, 160 acres of oats and
40 acres of barley, were destroyed by the king's army when
he lay about Berwick, and 100 oxen and cows were taken
by the Scots the night they came suddenly to Tweedmouth.'
Similar losses were incurred by Scots. One random example is
a freeholding in Paxton-on-Tweed consisting of a house, four
acres of arable land, five husband-lands of fifteen acres each,
two grassmen's holdings of pasture and two cottages: it was
worth £2 16s 8d 'in times of peace' but had become value-
less in 1315. The nuns of Coldstream had their sheep attacked
and their orchard destroyed by a marauding English army in
1296. However, they were unusually fortunate in being subsequently compensated. The north of the country also suffered
from marauding troops: Fordun stated that in 1337 'Gowrie,
Angus and Mearns was for the most part almost reduced to
a hopeless wilderness, and to utter want.' However, as wide-

spread and long lasting as the wars were, their effects should not be exaggerated. The only long-term effects were felt in the Borders, with the loss of Berwick and Roxburgh. In general, there was no lasting depopulation and the crops ruined by scorched-earth tactics could eventually be replenished.

War was only one of a number of disasters to have seriously affected the Scottish economy during the first half of the fourteenth century and fortunes were very different from the prosperity of 100 years earlier. That prosperity had been accompanied by a continuing population growth that had begun during the twelfth century which, in turn, entailed a huge demand for food. By 1300 in Central and Western Europe the amount of land under cultivation had reached a point that would not be matched for another five hundred years. Thus, the population had reached the maximum number capable of surviving on the land available. In many areas with a similar pressure on the land – notably Flanders, Champagne and parts of western Germany – there was a definitive move towards industrialisation whereby many urban areas were created. While Scotland shared in this population growth, it did not experience quite such un-comfortable overcrowding. By the 1340s the density of population around the Italian town of Pistoia had reached thirty-eight per square kilometre and this was by no means unusual either in the wider Tuscany area or further afield. Scotland's population had an average density of only eleven per square kilometre. Nevertheless, there was apparently some degree of pressure on the land, indicated by the extension of farming into hunting reserves. However, this was probably a relatively manageable situation, with sufficient unused land available which could be exploited to produce more food. Oats were being grown 1,100 feet up on Lammermuir, for example, with the result that the needs of the population could fairly easily be sustained. This was also the case in Sweden, Basse-Provence and Catalonia. The population in these areas would have to have risen proportionately far higher than the European norm to cause the same kinds of pressure experienced in areas with denser populations. This ability to exploit unused land had other ramifications in terms of the returns to be expected. In much of Europe the subsistence existence by which most people lived was exacerbated by the diminishing returns on the land. Crop rotation was seldom practised, causing the land to become quickly exhausted, drained of its goodness by the need to plant as many crops as often as possible rather than leaving some land fallow. This led to an overall decrease in the annual yield of grain, especially wheat (bread being the staple of the European diet). In the mid-thirteenth century a farmer could expect to recover at least six to eight grains from each seed sown (compared with the modern return of twenty). As the goodness of the land worsened, yields fell to as little as two to three grains per seed – a drop of as much as two thirds. This might have enabled the farmer to sustain the local population but he could ill afford to face any sort of crop failure.

Because there was not such an intense need to recycle every scrap of available land, Scotland's farmers perhaps fared a little better than many of their European counterparts. While the country's climate was not suited to the production of wheat, in those areas where the cereal was grown yields were good by medieval standards. A Scottish farmer could expect as much as four grains per seed, a particularly healthy yield in comparison with the mere two grains that was the norm in parts of Northern Europe. These better yields provided something of a cushion in times of crop failures, which occurred intermittently from the mid-twelfth century as a result of the worsening climate. Weather patterns for Northern Europe became generally wetter and cooler, marked by the so-called 'Little Ice Age', which heralded increasingly severe winters and wet summers. Scotland was no exception, though even within the country there was a marked variation between the wet, windy and less fertile west and the drier and more fertile east. The adverse weather conditions meant that throughout Europe cereal crops were decimated. The periodic destruction of wheat crops in England caused famines in 1272, 1277, 1283, 1292 and 1311. Poor harvest years were likewise recorded in Scotland intermittently from the 1260s onwards. These isolated examples proved surmountable but crop failures in successive years lessened the ability to recover. The famine of 1315-18 proved to be one of the most severe ever recorded in Western Europe, causing almost every country to lose virtually the whole of one harvest, often two or three. The lack of sun hindered the production of salt by evaporation and thus made it difficult to preserve what meat there was. The shortage of food caused great mortality across Europe: to cite one random example, 10 per cent of the population of Ypres died from starvation in these three years. The chronicle of Lanercost recorded that in 1316 'there was such a mortality of men in England and Scotland through famine... as has not been heard of in our time.' It was certainly severe:

Fordun (who may have misdated this famine, asserting that it occurred in 1310) commented that:

> so great was the famine and dearth of provisions in the kingdom of Scotland that, in most places many were driven, by the pinch of hunger, to feed on the flesh of horses and other unclean animals.

This desperate situation accorded with one English chronicler who recorded that people resorted to eating cats, dogs and even their own children. The late 1330s was another difficult period as, in addition to war and population pressure, Scotland probably suffered from monetary contraction, the indirect result of Edward III's efforts to finance a campaign against England's French enemies. Famine occurred then too: Wyntoun recorded a case of cannibalism in Perth. Nevertheless, the theory that Scotland did not have quite such dire problems of overcrowding as other areas of Europe prior to the Black Death provides a good example to back up the claim that medieval agriculture could support the population of the period and that, in fact, it could have fed many more mouths if required. Indeed, the traditional Malthusian interpretation of the Black Death – that it was nature's answer to a demographic crisis, arriving just in time to check a population spiralling wildly out of control – has increasingly been dismissed. The frequency of harvest failures and the high death rate resulting from serious food shortages, coupled with the finite amount of land available, served to check the natural growth in population and ensured that the level attained in the west remained fairly static throughout the century preceding the Black Death. Plague did not therefore merely precipitate an existing demographic trend. As precarious as the situation was, the fact remains that Europe had managed to sustain and stabilise its population long before the pandemic occurred. There is nothing to prove that it could not have continued to do so for an indefinite period had plague not broken out.

In any event, in late 1347 the Black Death arrived in Europe. By 1346 rumours were circulating amongst the major European seaports of a terrifying epidemic sweeping through the East: 'India was depopulated, Tartary, Mesopotamia, Syria, Armenia were covered with dead bodies; the Kurds fled in vain to the mountains. In Caramania and Caesarea none were left alive...'. The epidemic spread from marauding Tartars to Italian merchants trading in the port of Caffa who, in their hurry to escape the deadly outbreak, then unwittingly carried the disease back to Sicily and Genoa with them. 'In January of the year 1348', wrote a Flemish chronicler,

> three galleys put in at Genoa, driven by a fierce wind from the East, horribly infected and laden with a variety of spices and other valuable goods. When the inhabitants of Genoa learnt this, and saw how suddenly and irremediably they infected other people, they were driven forth from that port by burning arrows and divers engines of war; for no man dared touch them; nor was any man able to trade with them, for if he did he would be sure to die forthwith. Thus, they were scattered from port to port...

Their dispersal ensured the spread of the plague – within a month one expelled Genoese galley had arrived at the French port of Marseilles and, by the end of the year, the epidemic had reached Germany, Spain, and the south of England. Sometime in 1349 it reached the English soldiers stationed near the Scottish border. It arrived at a time when the populations of both nations were beleagured by years of social and economic dislocation caused by warfare, harvest

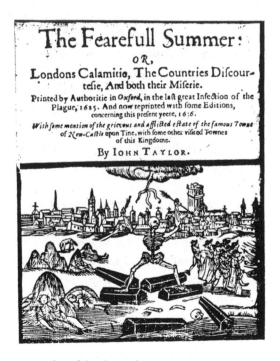

Contemporary woodcut of the plague of London: Contemporary depictions of the effects of plague provide a good indication of the horror and panic that outbreaks caused. This shows the devestation plague brought to London in 1665

failures, famines and outbreaks of animal diseases that further threatened the precarious food supplies. Moreover, Scotland had suffered severe military losses in recent years, particularly at the battle of Neville's Cross in 1346, as a result of which the nation's king had been taken prisoner. With the prevailing medieval consciousness which attributed such ominous portents as heralding large-scale disasters, it would not have been surprising if local people had expected some awful event to be imminent. Indeed, rumours of plague's proximity were beginning to cause alarm in the county of Durham by July 1349. This county was almost unique in England for showing evidence of panic spreading before the arrival of the disease, though this was probably significantly influenced by the concurrent devastation caused by the continuing hostilities with Scotland. Numerous instances were recorded of peasants being reluctant to take on the responsibility of any new land 'through fear of the plague.' Their fear proved to be justified: almost inevitably the Black Death arrived killing probably well over half the population of Billingham and the bishop's roll recorded that, in the village of West Thickley, all the tenants died. By the winter of 1349 English forces had carried plague over the border and the laughter of the Scottish soldiers upon hearing of their enemies' infection soon rang hollow. During 1350 Scotland faced the Black Death. According to the metrical version of Hector Boece's chronicle,

> *Sic pestilence rang ouir all Scotland,*
> *Richt venomous, quhilk smyttit hes so smart,*
> *Of the pepill deuorit the third part.*

The loss of up to a third of the population could have had little other than profound consequences. Throughout Europe the general pattern of change demonstrates what a devastating impact the Black Death and subsequent epidemics had on commerce, rents, wages and prices. The Scottish chronicler Walter Bower remembered a 'great fertility of victuals' in Robert III's reign (1390-1406). That neatly summarises the general situation in Europe during the second half of the fourteenth century. The drastic fall in population seriously altered the social structure, to the detriment of landlords and the benefit of tenants. There was less demand for food and land but more for labour, with the result that rents and prices fell while wages increased. For many of those who survived life was abundantly better than before the Black Death. Until the end of the fourteenth century repeated outbreaks of plague hindered the population's ability to recover, keeping living conditions better for many and ensuring a continuing demand for produce. One important point needs stressing: of course, the greater the mortality from plague, the more keenly these effects were manifested. In Scotland, where death rates were not so high, the post-plague situation in which Europe found itself did not have such serious repercussions. Similarly, the likelihood that subsequent outbreaks were localised and therefore less severe overall makes it probable that their cumulative effects did not repress population levels to quite the same extent. However, it must be remembered that demographic recovery did not noticeably begin until at least the mid-fifteenth century. Though comparatively spared, the nation nevertheless shared in the basic European post-plague trends.

The most obvious consequence of the Black Death was the drop in population, regardless of the exact percentage this may have been. Thus the desperate pressure for land and resources, so apparent during the preceding century, was immediately eased. Initially, at least, the population fall resulted in a profound reversal of fortunes for landlords and tenants, tipping the scales completely in favour of the latter, for whom life before the Black Death had generally been harsh. Firstly, it allowed them a greater degree of social mobility and standard of living. The shortage of labour meant the worker was able to demand higher wages and better conditions, and to pick and choose for whom he worked. If his current employer refused his demands he was able simply to travel in order to find someone who was prepared to offer a better deal. In the immediate aftermath of the epidemic this was perhaps restricted fairly much to movement within the wider vicinity. However, over time, workers began to seek better conditions further afield in England – another indication that the population fall (and thereby labour shortage) in Scotland was less dramatic than over the border – in spite of further, localised outbreaks. An indication of the severity of the outbreak in 1379, for example, is indicated by the alleged death of more than 6,000 inhabitants of Newcastle alone (whereas plague in Scotland that year merited hardly a mention by chroniclers). While Scots' migration south in search of employment was an established practice, their numbers before the Black Death had not apparently been large enough to be deemed a threat. In England, even before the plague, medieval travelling salesmen had often attracted criticism by competing for custom in smaller towns. During

the later fourteenth century, in the wake of intermittent outbreaks, migrant labour in search of inflated wages became the
target of even more legislation. In Northumberland Scottish
migrants became sufficiently numerous to be considered a
political threat, with government legislation being passed in
1398 for their removal south of the River Tyne. Scottish soldiers also found work in English employment, made possible
by the post-plague shortage of manpower. This trend peaked
in 1369-73, with the English force of 6,000 fighting in France
in 1373, apparently containing several hundred Scots. It may
be estimated that around a hundred Scots entered English
service annually during these years. For some this desire to
enter the military may have appeared all the more attractive
due to the absence in Scotland of paid armies, with troops
traditionally summoned through the fundamental obligation
of all able-bodied men to defend their country under the
charge of the nobility. Indeed, it has been argued that one
indirect consequence of the Black Death was the introduction of paid armies in the later fourteenth century, as magnates sought incentives to retain their tenants.

The situation for the landlord, therefore, was not a profitable one. Knighton noted their dilemma:

> the workmen were so puffed up and contrary-minded
> that… if anyone wanted to hire them he had to pay
> what they asked: either his fruit and crops rotted, or he
> had to give in to the workmen's arrogant andgreedy
> demands.

In England this was considered a serious enough problem by the government to necessitate national legislation. The Ordinance of Labourers, passed in 1349, was an attempt to freeze wages and prices at their pre-plague levels and, thereby, check inflation and restrict social mobility. Parliament realised that this would never be achieved so long as labourers were able to move freely from one employer to another in search of higher wages and so long as employers were free to tempt workers with advantageous offers. Therefore, the decree passed was designed to restrict an employee's ability to leave his current position, to compel him to accept any work offered to him, to prohibit employers from offering wages greater than those paid three years earlier and to fix the prices that butchers, bakers and fishmongers could charge. Both this and the subsequent Statute of Labourers of 1351 (which, in addition, sought to codify the wages of labourers and artisans) tended in practice to be ignored, though the 671 men employed before 1359 to enforce the legislation helped to ensure that, within a few years, wages had indeed fallen, albeit not to pre-plague levels. Fines were imposed on both employer and employee for the contravention of the statute. However, in the event, the majority of those punished were peasants and, while the laws may not solely have been intended for the repression of the peasantry, they could do little other than benefit landowners (employers) in thelong run.

In Scotland no such legislation was deemed necessary. This was not because the trend was not apparent but rather because the plague was less severe and therefore caused less of a labour shortage than elsewhere. Nevertheless, an indication that workers were able to demand higher wages is proved by circumstantial evidence that the situation for landowners worsened in the aftermath of the Black Death. Some explicit data for higher wages exists: in 1380, for example, three-quarters of the £18 9s 2d spent on the Strathearn demesne (estate) at Fowlis Wester was on labour: a phenomenally high proportion. The steep increase in labour costs made it more difficult for landowners to manage their lands and many became forced to lease them out in order that they should not fall into total neglect. James Douglas of Dalkeith had done so in Kilbucho and Aberdour by 1376; by 1380 the extent of the Earl of Strathearn's demesne had been significantly reduced (and completely rented out by 1445) while all Cupar Angus Abbey's demesnes were leased over the same period.

Landowners' impoverishment was furthered by their tenants being able to demand this land at significantly reduced rents. Knighton noted both trends, commenting that landlords 'remitted the payment of rents lest their tenants should quit for want of labour' and 'either gave [their lands] up altogether, or manage them in a looser way, at a low rent, lest their tenements should fall into utter and irredeemable decay, and the land everywhere lie wholly unworked.' While the fortunes of the landlord clearly took a turn for the worse, the tenant's situation greatly improved. He could now demand higher wages and lease more lands at rents lower than ever before. Thus, a change in the structure of landholdings was instigated. The rental from the Douglas of Dalkeith estate indicates larger peasant holdings: each husbandman probably had at least four oxgangs (nominally 52 acres) compared with only one or two on late thirteenth-century estates. National land assessments were revised in 1366, after the second plague outbreak, and indicate a sharp fall in rents throughout the country: excluding Argyll (where the returns are incomplete) the total fell from a thirteenth-century level of £45,575 to £23,826 – practically half the value. Contemporaries might have blamed the wars for the fall in rents, noting that the old assessment values were 'in times of peace.' But there was no direct correlation between cheaper rents and combat zones: the north (44 per cent) declined almost as much as the south (52 per cent).

Neither could this be attributed to deflation resulting from monetary contraction, which occurred increasingly during the later fourteenth century. This was partly a result of the continued payments the Scots were to make to the English for David II's ransom, amounting to over £50,000 between 1357 and 1377. This must have considerably affected the nation's total money supply of £130,000-£180,000. The 20 per cent fall in the weight of Scottish coins in the fifty years prior to the Black Death continued to fall a further 15 per cent by 1367. Moreover, Scottish currency became increasingly devalued against the English pound: between 1320 and 1333 the Scots pound was the equivalent of 5,143 grains of silver, dropping to 4,320 grains in 1351 (the immediate aftermath of the Black Death). After 1400 the Scottish pound was equal to only 1,680 grains of silver. By this time the term 'usual money of Scotland' had become common, reflecting an acknowledgement that Scots coins had become worth only half as much as their English equivalents. In England, while the weight of the pound was the same as Scotland in 1351, from 1412 its silver content was still as high as 3,600 grains. Though the scarcity of bullion was regularly bemoaned in parliament, Scotland was merely in line with the situation throughout Europe. Scottish devaluation, though much worse than in England, was no worse than in commercially renowned Milan and less severe than in Castile. While a shortage of money in the economy would depress rents, it would most likely have made prices fall fairly evenly, but this did not happen. Therefore, it might be concluded that population fall is the likeliest explanation, especially given the trend towards larger holdings.

However, population fall alone would not necessarily have had such effect. If peasant mobility had been restricted through serfdom, landlords would have been better able to maintain cheap labour and high rents. But serfdom had virtually disappeared from Scottish society by the mid-fourteenth century, resulting largely from a combination of a rising population being less tied to a particular landlord and the social dislocation caused by the Wars of Independence. A minority of tenants were freeholders, holding their land in perpetuity through 'feudal leases' from their landlord. This provided a greater degree of security than the annual renewable lease, the basis by which the majority rented: to cite one random example, of the 119 leases on the estate of James Douglas of Dalkeith in 1376-77, 108 were for one year. Short-term leases, though less secure and a disincentive to agricultural improvement, allowed for a social division between those tenants who held them. Some enjoyed the higher status of husbandmen, allowing them to hold touns individually or jointly, cultivate the arable land and graze sheep and cattle on communal pastures. The majority of peasant tenants were cottars or grassmen. Some were fortunate enough to have several acres of their own but most were simply subtenants, holding only a small piece of land from husbandmen in return for working in the latter's fields. The Scottish system, which emphasised short-term leases, benefited the tenant rather than the landlord in the event of a serious population fall such as that which occurred after the Black Death. The disappearance of serfdom left landlords vulnerable as tenants would only then stay on their land if rents were lowered. The Douglas of Dalkeith rental indicates this: tenants who did not bother to negotiate their rents were charged at their pre-plague level.

Aside from enjoying higher wages and more land at lower rents, tenant farmers were also particularly able to benefit from the economic climate in the wake of the Black Death. The general pattern throughout Europe in the immediate post-plague years was one of generally falling prices caused by the supply of goods outstripping demand. The disposable income now available to peasants meant that they could afford some luxury items that their subsistence existence had previously denied them, with the result that, while the price of staple goods fell, the demand for (and price of) luxury goods rose. Though temporary, the consequent demand for wool and leather particularly benefited Scotland, as climatic and geophysical factors dictated that the country's medieval agriculture was based more on pastoral rather than arable farming. Pastoral farming predominated in the Highlands and the southern uplands, where the terrain was rugged and the soil poor. Fordun described the agriculture of the country:

In the upland districts, and along the highlands, the fields are less productive, except only in oats and barley. The country is, there, very hideous, interspersed with moors and marshy fields, muddy and dirty; it is, however, full of pasturage grass for cattle, and comely with verdure in the glens, along the water-courses. This region abounds in wool-bearing sheep, and in horses; and its soil is grassy, feeds cattle and wild beasts, is rich in milk and wool, and manifold in its wealth of fish, in sea, river, and lake.

Even the areas of poorer quality soil were therefore by no means unprofitable in comparison to the more fertile coastal areas in the east, which Fordun described as:

pretty level and rich, with green meadows, and fertile and productive fields of corn and barley, and well adapted for growing beans, peas and all other produce; destitute, however, of wine and oil, though by no means so of honey and wax.

Throughout the Middle Ages the nation's trade was essentially local, with peasants from the surrounding countryside selling their produce at the burgh market. Here they also obtained cash to pay the rent and purchased clothing, tools and pottery from the burgh's craftsmen. Burghs were invariably founded for financial gain, a fact recognised through the large amount of clauses dealing with mercantile issues in early burgh legislation. The burgh was, after all, a community organised for the undertaking of trade and the merchants of each had a monopoly on trading rights. Only they were allowed to buy and sell all merchandise within the kingdom, a privilege confirmed by a charter of David II in 1364. In order to participate in (and hence benefit from) this commercial monopoly, citizenship had to be earned, usually through the demonstration of financial solvency. Burghs were the focus of the nation's commercial life, but they naturally relied on the countryside for their economic success. Edinburgh, Aberdeen, Perth and Dundee were the 'four great towns of Scotland', acknowledged in a proclamation from Bruges, then the staple port through which Scotland's trade passed, in 1348 – when the Black Death had already broken out across much of Europe but was yet to reach Scotland. Each of these towns benefited from jurisdiction over a large, relatively fertile area: Edinburgh, in particular, had a trading monopoly over a vast hinterland stretching almost to the English border and it is no coincidence that it was the richest and most prolific burgh in the kingdom.

Though it only accounted for a small proportion of Scotland's gross domestic product, international trade was also undertaken, channelled through the royal burghs, especially Edinburgh, Aberdeen, Perth, Dundee, Linlithgow and Haddington. Fourteenth-century Scotland's trading partners included Scandinavia, northern Germany, France, the Low Countries and, clandestinely in wartime, England and Ireland. The nation's main exports, due to the country's pastoral economy, were wool, woolfells (sheepskins) and hides, as well as fish (particularly salmon). Scottish production of these was both prolific and renowned. Melrose Abbey and the Earl of Douglas both had approximately 15,000 sheep, making them among the most prolific sheep farmers in Europe. Indeed, wool from Melrose was sufficiently renowned to be included in a list of 'British' wool prices from the Flemish town of Douai around 1270. The quality of North Sea fish was also famous: as early as the thirteenth century the word *l'abberdan* (Aberdeen) was synonymous with cod throughout much of North-Western Europe. Imports, on the other hand, mainly consisted of manufactured goods and those, such as wheat, of which climatic conditions hindered domestic cultivation. In the thirteenth century wheat (for upper-class and urban consumption) was usually imported from Ireland, though war with England and the conversion of much Irish land from arable to pasture put paid to that and Scotland had to look elsewhere to make up its shortfall in grain production. Although England was a profitable source, war made this unreliable. Therefore, France and the Baltic became favoured. Other imports consisted largely of manufactured goods, including quality cloth and pottery, armour and military equipment and wine.

The basic pattern of Scotland's foreign trade – exporting raw materials and importing manufactured goods – implies an undeveloped economy. But this would not be a strictly accurate conclusion to draw: the importance of Scotland's wool ('the medieval equivalent of North Sea oil', as Alexander Grant called it) must not be underestimated. The importance of the wool trade had social ramifications, as sheep farming afforded the peasantry a share of the national wealth. The demand for wool naturally worked most to the advantage of those landowners who owned the bigger flocks, but they were not the only ones to benefit. Better-off husbandmen were also able to take advantage: fifteenth-century legislation prohibited them from wearing the expensive coloured cloth traditionally reserved for the upper classes and the booming wool trade during the fourteenth century meant that a substantial number of peasants would have been able to own various luxuries in the period before the Black Death as well.

This is not to imply that the Scottish economy had no problems to contend with prior to the mid-fourteenth century. The intermittent famines that struck Europe in the century or so before 1350 entailed a drop in productivity and demand, which had a detrimental impact on commerce. For Scotland, it would appear that the main disruption to trade during the first half of the fourteenth century was war, both internally and with England. Over this period the weight of Scottish coins fell by 20 per cent, due in part to the £20,000 'payment for peace' that was imposed by the Treaty of Edinburgh in 1328. Hostilities inevitably disrupted (though did not halt) trade, not only with England itself but also with other countries, such as Ireland, through English-imposed blockades. Wool and leather, the mainstay of the export industry, were hit hard. Between 1327 and 1332, the period from which the earliest figures survive, Scotland exported an annual average of 5,700 sacks of wool and 36,100 leather hides. That the wars took their toll is evidenced by the subsequent fall in these amounts a decade later: 2,450 wool sacks and 17,900 hides for the period 1341-42 to 1342-43. Moreover, the realities of war ensured that much valuable land was laid waste, especially in the Borders, due to marauding forces and the employment of scorched-earth tactics. War, therefore, had adversely affected the economy before the Black Death struck.

Although Scotland's economy certainly suffered due to a combination of war and famine well before the epidemic broke out, this should not be exaggerated. In the ongoing debate as to whether war or plague played a more important role in fourteenth-century economic fortunes, the latter should be considered the greater instigator of change. While war had an adverse effect on productivity and trade, these aspects were surmountable. Crops could be resown and livestock replenished, trade undertaken clandestinely (as indeed it was). But the loss of perhaps a third of the population from the Black Death entailed a third less demand and a third fewer labourers to tend the land and harvest crops: in other words, a third fewer producers and consumers upon whom commercial activity depended. The first statistical evidence of a decline in Scottish exports is evident from the later fourteenth-century customs accounts rather than from the years of Anglo-Scottish conflict before David II's release from English captivity in 1357, an indication that plague, not war, more radically affected commercial fortunes.

Post-plague prices from 1358-84, which may be compared with those from the period 1326-31, reveal a steep increase in the price of wheat and malt, little change in oats and meal and a drop in the value of cattle and sheep. The drop in the value of sheep and cattle indicates that after the Black Death livestock farming became the increasing trend, partly because it could be undertaken on land of poorer quality and was less labour intensive. This last factor meant that it was probably the case that only livestock farming remained profitable for landlords. Grain production was carried out on the best land and must have contracted roughly in line with the population fall, which explains the increase in its value. Arable farming began to expand again only around the mid-fifteenth century into lands which, since 1350, had been used for grazing. The post-Black Death trend for pastoral farming was also influenced by the continuing deterioration of the climate which meant that oats would not ripen at such high altitudes as before those grown so high up in the Lammermuir hills could no longer be harvested. That the post-plague demand for wool and leather benefited Scotland is reflected in the customs accounts for the later fourteenth century. The 1370s and 1380s was the zenith of the country's wool and leather exports: between 1370 and 1374 annual wool exports averaged 7,360 sacks, compared to 5,460 annually during each of the previous five years. Indeed, in 1372 wool exports from England (one of Scotland's commercial competitors) were subject to government restrictions, leading to a demand from foreign manufacturers for Scottish wool: 9,252 sacks were exported that year (plus 1,875 sacks of English wool smuggled through Scotland). This indicates that such an amount must have been clipped from Scotland's two and a quarter million sheep regularly and that the difference – 2,000 sacks – must normally have been used in domestic cloth manufacture, which implies that Scotland had a respectable cloth industry. The foreign demand for wool and leather was even more profitable considering the low price sheep and cattle fetched at domestic market. Though figures are not available for the years immediately preceding the Black Death, those from two decades earlier exist to

provide an indication of general price trends. Both commod-
ities depreciated considerably in value – sheep were worth
2s in 1330 but only half that amount in 1368 – and cattle fell
from 7s in 1331 to 5s in 1358.

However, the economic boom proved to be temporary,
as the continuing population fall could not sustain demand
indefinitely. By the end of the fourteenth century Europe was
entering an economic recession, in which Scotland shared. In
the late 1380s the country's annual wool exports had declined
to an average of just over 3,100 sacks and, from 1400 to
1420, they averaged about 2,600 annually, with some individual years' totals being considerably lower. Leather exports
remained healthy for slightly longer: between 1380 and 1384
they averaged 56,400 hides per year, falling only slightly
over the next five years to an annual average of 48,300. By
the end of the fourteenth century this figure had dropped
even further, to 34,200, and the trend continued well into
the fifteenth century. Producers suffered greatly as a consequence. Even the renowned wool from Melrose Abbey did
not always remain in high demand: in 1404 only thirty sacks
were exported, almost half the normal amount. Prices rose as
a result of this downturn and concurrent monetary devaluation, causing the abbot of Dunfermline to lament in 1409 that
'all things are dearer than they were in times past.' Likewise
rents increased, as did land values. By the 1420s land assessment was returning to thirteenth-century levels, implying a
doubling in valuations since the revision of 1366. The gross
rental of Strathearn rose by 40 per cent between 1340 and
1445 while many of the Douglas of Dalkeith rentals in the
early fifteenth century were 10-25 per cent higher than in

1376-77. Landowners throughout Europe experienced the same reversal in fortunes.

Thus, it might at first sight appear that, within fifty years of the Black Death, the status quo within Scotland and Europe was restored, with landlords' fortunes recovering as rents and prices rose and wages fell, tenants reverting to their miserable existences and the natural population recovery in the wake of plague being just around the corner. This, however, would be too simplistic a picture. To begin with, it ignores the external factors that also affected economic fluctuations. It is impossible to disentangle the effects of plague from the effects of war and doubtless much land depreciation occurred as a result of continued warfare rather than rent decreases and wage increases after the Black Death. In explaining fluctuations in land values for the century after the 1340s, we must take into account the intermittent resumption of hostilities both internally and, from the 1380s, with England. This occurred particularly in the south of Scotland, with Berwickshire, Roxburghshire, Teviotdale and Annandale variously under English occupation. In 1384 an invading English force destroyed Haddington and the following year much of Lothian was ravaged under the personal command of the English king Richard II. Both events very probably adversely affected the nearby Dalkeith estates, one of the few areas for which comparable figures survive. The north also suffered, predominantly as a result of internal hostilities caused by the rule of Robert II's son Alexander, the 'Wolf of Badenoch.' His burning of Elgin Cathedral in 1390 is the most notorious example of his destruction and, though data do not survive for the area, it is probable that considerable depreciation occurred as a result of such action. Furthermore, there was no direct correlation between trade levels and plague outbreaks to indicate the extent to which epidemics themselves affected commercial activity. More-over, it was not the straightforward case that every landlord suffered in the wake of the Black Death. In Scotland there is evidence to indicate that the comparatively low death rates meant that the nobility generally fared rather better than their counterparts elsewhere, not least in terms of their own rates of mortality. The myriad hardships that the shortage of labour entailed – caused by the Black Death – were certainly experienced by landowners, but probably to a lesser extent. Nobles' finances were certainly affected and even after the rise in valuations during the later fourteenth century they probably still lagged behind inflation. The temporary boom in wool and leather exports during the 1370s and 1380s would have been only of fleeting compensation, even to those landowners who owned huge flocks or herds.

In England nobles sought to counter such financial pressures through the various material gains to be had from war, the accumulation of larger estates and the acquisition of royal patronage. In Scotland none of these options was quite so profitable. It was more difficult for the Scottish nobility to profit directly from warfare due to the lack of standing armies: nobles suffered as much as gained from cross-border raiding, not least due to the lack of territory available to conquer. The acquisition of royal patronage was also less profitable as the Crown was comparatively less well off. While Robert II (1371-90) and Robert III (1390-1406) were prolific in their granting of annuities to both the nobility and the Church (their patronage could total over £2,000 a year, four times David II's annual average in the 1360s), the amounts paled in comparison with their English counterparts – £1,300 in the early 1400s as against the £30,000 then paid out by Henry IV. Comparisons aside, Scottish royal finances were generally stable, in spite of the necessary payments toward David II's ransom after 1357. Indeed, in 1374, after the books had been balanced, the Crown could boast a healthy surplus of £1,800 from a total income that year of just over £14,000. Its revenue, prior to the later fourteenth century, was largely derived from land and customs and was, therefore considerably at the mercy of prevailing economic conditions. Despite this, the balance of income and expenditure was generally maintained and, although these naturally fluctuated, it was in a generally complementary way. In the mid-thirteenth century Crown lands yielded something in the region of £5,000 annually but Robert Bruce and David II's policy of providing supporters with grants significantly reduced their net value. Revenue fell to around £2,000 a year in the late 1320s and only £500 after 1365. Customs yields, on the other hand, were about £2,000 in the late 1320s, when the main rate was 6s 8d for a sack of wool. David II's ransom caused this rate to treble in 1358 and quadruple ten years later, to £1 6s 8d per sack. This greatly increased revenue – it averaged £7,000 a year during the 1360s, £10,000 after 1368, at a time when the nation's exports were booming. Crown finances had, therefore, come to be based almost entirely on the income from customs, which entailed a reversal of fortunes when exports slumped in the early fifteenth century. During the fifteenth century, in a reversal of fourteenth-century policy, monarchs increasingly forfeited or retained lands, probably for fiscal reasons.

With regard to the third option, inheritance patterns in Scotland made it difficult to accumulate territory, although in this respect nobles differed little from their English and French counterparts. Estates were normally heritable, in other words, they passed from father to eldest son if possible. This was a precarious system: between 1300 and 1469 every twenty-five year generation (with only one exception) witnessed at least a quarter of the families fail in the direct male line. Between 1350 and 1374 the failure rate was as high as 47 per cent, although to what extent plague was at all a factor in this would be purely conjectural. Certainly it would seem likely that, compared to the rest of society, the nobility was less affected by the Black Death. Daughters (and thereby their husbands) might receive the land if no sons were available, though frequently a more distant male relation would be favoured. The pattern of inheritance among the nobility, therefore, was one of dispersal over several generations or enlargement by indirect inheritance. Among other magnates (those at the top of society) the same pattern was apparent. Of forty-seven important families during the 1350s and 1360s, thirteen had died out by 1400. However, this is consistent with the pre-plague pattern: of forty-two prominent families from the 1320s fourteen had died out in the direct male line by 1350. While the majority of the Scottish nobility conformed to the general pattern in England and France, the same cannot be said for the country's lesser nobles. During the mid-fourteenth century the greater barons were also not producing enough heirs to replace them completely;

however, male replacement rates did become positive in the 1380s. From this time over a third survived beyond 1469, in direct contrast to England and France, thereby restricting the inheritance of land to a smaller body of baronial families. While these enabled the accumulation of territory through direct inheritance, many noble families produced too few sons to ensure that estates remained strictly within the family.

The evidence indicates that Scottish nobles were not so financially affected by plague despite having higher labour costs and lower land values. Using figures for the early fifteenth century to indicate trends, it seems likely that most magnates received the equivalent of £500,000 (tax free) a year – a healthy amount and a great deal more than the average tenant, who probably considered £10 a comfortable annual income (in the region of £10,000 in today's terms). They generally retained sufficient funds to allow solvency: indeed, some could be ostentatious. There was a building boom between 1380 and 1500, with much lavish expenditure going on properties such as Hermitage Castle in Roxburghshire. Tower-houses flourished, an impressive example being Threave in Galloway, built by Archibald 'the Grim', third Earl of Douglas with clearly no concern for its cost. The castle built by David II in Edinburgh cost £758 between 1367 and 1383 – under £50 a year – which was fairly typical and affordable to most nobles. Castles were necessary for providing somewhere 'for the safe-keeping of (his) people and (his) goods', as William Keith stated in 1394 when building Dunnottar, near Stonehaven. Nobles could also amass considerable fortunes: although in the wake of the Black Death James Douglas of Dalkeith's lands declined steeply in value, ten years later his rental (covering approximately half his estate) was worth £483, which indicates that the total income from rents was probably in the region of £900. Similarly, the revenue from the Earl of Mar's estates totalled £1,000-1,300. By way of comparison, the average annual income a contemporary English earl could expect was 1,000 marks (£667). While the lack of statistics makes it difficult to ascertain whether they were typical of their peers, in the later fourteenth century Dalkeith and Mar were hardly impoverished. Indeed, on his death in 1392 Dalkeith bequeathed a vast array of possessions, including four sets of armour, numerous items of gold jewellery, expensive silks and furs, various books and religious relics. The items together were worth £1,559 – a considerable sum by any nobleman's standards. A further indication that the nobility's fortunes could remain healthy is provided by their continued investment in cultural pursuits, a trend which seems at odds with the traditional picture of aristocratic economic crisis in the wake of plague. While cultural investment cannot be determined precisely for the immediate aftermath of the epidemic, it is perhaps nevertheless significant that fifteenth-century aristocrats invested just as much in lavish cultural pursuits as their thirteenth-century counterparts. The nobility's relative wealth, even in the difficult decades after the Black Death, is perhaps another indication that Scotland did not suffer so badly from plague as the rest of Europe.

That Scotland was less affected is also apparent from a social change that occurred elsewhere in the wake of plague. In England and France, perhaps partly as a result of the laws which prevented their taking advantage of the mobility the Black Death allowed them, there was evidence of widespread discontent among the peasant classes. In England this became manifested in the Peasants' Revolt of 1381 and in France in the Jacquerie of 1359. It should not be assumed that the Black Death alone 'caused' these uprisings, as insensitive taxation and feudal burdens played their part: neither can it be said that these risings would not have taken place had the Black Death not occurred. However, it may be concluded that the denial to the peasantry of the favourable circumstances that the Black Death instigated played an important role in the bitterness and tension that resulted in the following decades. In Scotland, however, peasant discontent was completely unapparent in the wake of the Black Death, which may be partly a reflection of the relatively low death rate. It is, however, indicative of other particularly Scottish conditions, as the nation did not experience the class tension that underlay the peasant uprisings in France and England. To begin with, Scottish society was not static insofar as the division between and among the lower nobility and higher peasantry was indistinct, a fluidity that was further aided by the crown's generally even-handed treatment of society as a whole. Those at the lower end of the social scale had no particular reason to be aggrieved: this was due in part to the elimination of serfdom, which elsewhere was promoted in the aftermath of the Black Death, making the peasant situation less stable. Moreover, the Scottish system of short leases also made it more difficult to impose high rents, as tenants were able to go elsewhere in the aftermath of plague. Another factor was the lack of standing armies, which eliminated the problem apparent in France of dissatisfaction among non-nobles who resented their being taxed to fund the war effort while nobles were exempted in return for military service. The French defeats of the 1350s exacerbated this situation and the taxation issue was a cause of bitter resentment. This meant that the gap between nobles and peasants widened, especially as it united the peasant classes against the upper echelons of society during the later fourteenth century. With regard to Scotland, Alexander Grant also argues persuasively that peasant consciousness was focused on foreign rather than domestic enemies, rather like medieval Switzerland, where peasant revolts were also absent. With the fourteenth century dominated by the Anglo-Scottish conflict, national consciousness extended throughout society, not least because husbandmen made up the bulk of Scottish armies. John Barbour's epic poem *The Brus* (1375) equated freedom from serfdom with freedom from foreign subjection and contained several stories of individual peasants taking their stance against the English.

The even-handed government of the country also played a part in the absence of class tensions. The immediate cause of the revolt in England was sustained taxation resulting in the imposition of a severe poll tax. In Scotland, however, the needs of royal finance affected the common people less than in other countries, because revenue mostly came from the rent of Crown lands (including royal burghs) and from customs on wool and leather exports. Taxes could be levied whenever circumstances demanded, but this was minimal. Direct taxes were levied on the people of Scotland infrequently during the fourteenth century – in 1326-30, 1341,

1358-60, 1365-66, 1368, 1370, 1373 and 1399. These 'contributions' constituted a shilling or so in the pound on the assessed value of individual property. The only heavy tax levied during the fourteenth century was a result of the 'payment for peace' of 1328 (£20,000 over three years). Neither could the king impose taxation for his own benefit unchecked – parliament had the final say in their ratification, as happened, for example, in 1368, when they decided that it was 'not expedient to the community to impose any contributions' the following year. Generally, tax yielded only around £2,000, making fiscal demands relatively small. Perhaps wary of events south of the border, there seemed to be a conscious effort not to impose a heavy and unpopular poll tax: in 1409 the governor, Albany, rejected a proposal to pay for the dismantling of Jedburgh castle through the imposition of a hearth tax, 'lest the poor folk should curse him.' There was no incentive for peasant society to be unduly dissatisfied with their situation and, therefore, no need for any rebellious movement.

In discussing the issue of government it might be expected that the Black Death would have had a profound impact not only on nationwide policy regarding the economy and so forth, but also on the running of everyday affairs. In Scotland this might be particularly expected given that the outbreak occurred at such a precarious time. The king had been captured after the battle of Neville's Cross in 1346, four years before plague struck, and was not released by the English until 1357. Absent from his realm, David II was unable to personally oversee government, an important requirement for effective medieval kingship. The presence of the king was deemed of great importance: he was the charismatic figurehead of the nation, providing an essential focus for the national community. It might be expected that this would have had severe consequences for the running of government in general and that a disaster such as the Black Death would have overturned what little vestment of effective government there was. However, despite this there is no direct evidence that the rule of the country was plunged into chaos with the outbreak of plague. Indeed, after David's return in 1357 a more rigorous and better-organised system of government gradually emerged, with annual exchequer audits taking place, often in the presence of the king, and the creation of the office of king's secretary. Aside from the king, Scotland's main institutions of government were the parliament and the less formal great councils (known as councils-general by the 1360s), both of which were composed of nobles, clergy and burgh representatives. Meeting irregularly but on average once a year (at various royal burghs but increasingly in Edinburgh), they oversaw the kingdom's major affairs. Parliaments enacted statute law, ratified treaties, supervised defence, justice and crown finance and whatever else was required in the national interest. Day-to-day business was carried out by the king and his privy (secret, or in other words, close-knit) council, whose members were drawn from the nobility and clergy. Their work was supplemented by a series of lesser bodies, which dealt with specific aspects of government such as financial and legal matters. Governments or councils, composed largely of prominent influential local families, ran affairs at the local level. While this could cause conflict, relations between the Crown and the nobility were generally good throughout the twelfth and thirteenth centuries. Government tended to be less centralised than in countries such as England, with the result that there were no real constitutional crises from the time of the Magna Carta onwards. The few rebellions by members of the nobility that occurred (such as that in 1363 instigated by the three men who had run the country in David II's absence) were largely personal attempts to gain greater powers and were inconsequential insofar as they were suppressed. The Crown's essential functions, generally carried out satisfactorily, were to ensure the nation's defence and the effective implementation of law and order: 'to make justice be done, and uphold the laws, and to defend the realm with whatever royal power is needed against the enemy's invasion attempts', as the Earl of Fife's tasks were laid down when he became guardian of the realm in 1388. This position was an important one – it essentially replaced the monarch in his minority, absence or (in the above case) incapacity and the responsibility on the man (or men) awarded it was enormous. In the event of David II's capture in 1346 this duty was handed to Robert Stewart, one of the country's leading magnates, who had led the retreat at Neville's Cross. He had already proved himself as an effective lieutenant in David's minority and his governance of the realm was successful during the 1350s as well. He was aided in this by the co-operation of William Douglas and Patrick Dunbar, members of two of Scotland's leading families, ensuring a good degree of political stability despite the disaster of Neville's Cross. During the subsequent eleven years of David's captivity, parliament continued to hold meetings regularly in the name of the absent king, despite the outbreak of the Black Death. Judicial and other ad hoc committees also date from the late 1360s, being elected to 'hold the parliament' in the absence of the majority of parliament due, in 1367, to the harvest and, in 1369, to bad weather. Similar committees met in 1370 and 1372, none of which correlate to plague years. The fact that parliament was disrupted due to adverse weather but not to plague provides a further indication that the outbreak caused no disruption to the running of government.

Indeed, the government of the country remained fairly stable throughout the second half of the fourteenth century, characterised by peaceful crown-magnate relations. David died in 1371, to be succeeded by Robert II (1371-90), whose reign Bower remembered as a time of 'tranquility and prosperity of peace.' This was in spite of the king's nepotism, whereby the Stewarts came to dominate the higher nobility: his sons came to possess eight out of fifteen earldoms. The other leading families were similarly endowed to ensure an even balance at the top of noble society. Robert was fortunate in that during his reign the country was reaping the benefits of the post-Black Death economic situation: trade was booming, with wool exports at an all-time high, and an outbreak of plague in 1379-80 was sufficiently localised as to have little impact. Old age (and a power struggle within his own family) forced him to relinquish power to his son, Robert, Earl of Fife in 1388, a position he effectively maintained until 1399 despite the accession of Robert II's eldest son John, Earl of Carrick, in 1390. Styled Robert III, his reign was dominated by the issue of guardianship, as he continued to be dogged by the illness and infirmity which had seen him give up his appointment, on behalf of his father, as lieutenant in 1384. The Duke of Rothesay proved to be inept as leader for, while his lieutenancy appeared successful, he managed to alienate much of the nobility and anger the wider political community through tactlessness and arrogance. His three-year 'contract' as guardian was not renewed in 1402 and the Earl of Fife, who had been raised to the Duke of Albany in 1398, was soon reinstated as lieutenant-general. In spite of the internal wrangling that entailed numerous guardians in a relatively short period, Robert III's reign was remarkable for not being more disastrous. Although Bower described him as 'the worst of kings and most miserable of men', the political squabbling during his reign never descended into civil war. Scottish kingship in the fifty years after the Black Death was beset by infirmity, captivity and internal power struggles, yet overall the country was satisfactorily governed. Whether due to competent leadership or to the fact that subsequent outbreaks were localised – probably more the latter – the Black Death of 1350 did not have any noticeable effect on the government of Scotland.

The population decline brought about by this severe outbreak of plague has been credited with accelerating the so-called 'Highland problem' that was to play an important part in domestic politics particularly during the fifteenth century. During the first half of the fourteenth century there was little apparent division between the Highlands and Lowlands. Though much of the land lying north of the Forth/Clyde Valley was composed of rugged terrain and poor soil, this was little different from some areas in the south of the country and simply entailed an emphasis on pastoral, rather than arable, farming (particularly of cattle rather than sheep). The geophysical aspects did not prevent settlement, though the area was more sparsely populated overall than the rest of the country. Neither was there a significant linguistic divide in the early fourteenth century, as Gaelic was spoken as far east as Fife and as far south as the River Clyde and Galloway. Gradually, however, a distinction began to emerge, of which Fordun, writing in the 1380s, gives an early example:

> The manners and customs of the Scots vary with the diversity of their speech. For two languages are spoken amongst them, the Scottish and the Teutonic; the latter of which is the language of those who occupy the seabird and plains, while the race of Scottish speech inhabits the highlands and outlying islands. The people of the coast are of domestic and civilised habits, trusty, patient, and urbane, decent in their attire, affable and peaceful, devout in Divine worship, yet always ready to resist a wrong at the hands of their enemies. The highlanders and people of the islands, on the other hand, are a savage and untamed race, rude and independent, given to rapine, ease-loving, clever and quick to learn, comely in person, but unsightly in dress, hostile to the English people and language, and, owing to diversity of speech, even to their own nation, and exceedingly cruel. They are, however, faithful and obedient to their king and country, and easily made to submit to law, if properly governed.

The distinction between the two areas was possibly accentuated by the Black Death – the death rate was probably proportionately less in the Highlands than the rest of Scotland due to the comparative sparseness of the population. The reduced population pressure on the land presumably seriously lessened – or even stopped – the continuing advance of people into the Highlands from the east and south. Furthermore, it was no longer necessary to farm the poor hilly areas of the south, with the result that differences in Highland and Lowland agriculture became more apparent. Changes in the linguistic balance further helped to accentuate the division between the two areas – the English language had been pushing back the frontiers of Gaelic since the eleventh century until, in the later fourteenth century, the latter was mainly confined to the Highlands and western isles. Its retreat halted during the fifteenth century and it became sustained: in the 1520s the chronicler John Major reckoned that 'half of Scotland' spoke it. The easing of population pressure in English-speaking areas (Lowlands), due in part to plague outbreaks, was most likely a factor, as population levels did not really begin to recover until at least the middle of the fifteenth century.

In themselves neither linguistic nor geographical differences made effective rule impossible. But there was an added dimension that did affect successful government, namely lawlessness. Increasingly there was a perceived division between 'wild' (Highland) and 'domestic' (Lowland) Scots. This division, however, had emerged by the middle of the fourteenth century: in other words, the Black Death did not instigate it. On the other hand, the differences in settlement patterns, agricultural viability and language may have helped to accelerate it: references to the problem of governing the Highlands appear in parliamentary records from 1369 onwards. This may have stemmed partly from the importance attached in Scotland to local rule due to the decentralised nature of the country's government. In the burghs local councils oversaw day-to-day affairs, while in the countryside the highest position of landownership carried with it similar duties (though, by the end of the fourteenth century, titles no longer guaranteed land and became instead honorific, as was already the case in England). Landholdings consisted of earldoms and provincial lordships, and the twenty-nine which existed during Robert I's reign were in the hands of thirteen earls and five provincial lords. Traditionally, these corresponded to provinces of the country, with the earls of each essentially acting as provincial rulers. The lordship of the Isles had been in the possession of the Macdonald clan since at least the twelfth century and their semi-autonomous control of the western seaboard from their power base in Islay occasioned antagonistic relations with the Scottish crown, not least through their expedient support of the English. Fordun's statement that Highlanders would be 'easily made to submit to law, if properly governed' hints that this was then not the case (in Lowland eyes, at least). Gaelic society maintained a distinct system of organisation which emphasised loyalty borne out of kinship over the concept of feudal obedience that had been introduced by twelfth-century kings following the Anglo-French tradition. (It should be noted that there was no absolute dichotomy, with much intermarriage between Highland and Lowland families and elements of both traditions combined: indeed, Robert II's daughter, Margaret, had married John Macdonald, the Lord of the Isles, in 1350.) In the fourteenth century, the particular brand of Gaelic 'feudalism', which operated more by the forcible takeover of territory, imposition of 'protection rackets' and plundering of rivals, was disrupted by a combination of the Scottish civil wars and the dying out of several major families. The Macdonald lordship of the Isles emerged as a semi-autonomous governing body which, like many ruling powers, sought territorial expansion as well as internal stabilisation. This precipitated a power struggle with the crown until their official forfeiture in 1493 (though their rule continued, in practice, for another five decades). A similar struggle also occurred in Moray, an area in the north of the country that had long been in opposition to the Scottish crown. For much of the period the area was controlled by three families, the Murrays, Randolphs and the Earls of Ross but, by the later fourteenth century, each of these families had died out in the male line. Robert II's third son Alexander (the 'Wolf of Badenoch') emerged victorious in the subsequent struggle for supremacy but he succeeded only in undermining rather than sustaining law and order in the region. Aside from his notorious burning of Elgin Cathedral in 1390, in the course of his 'rule' he also saw his sons undertake a massive raid into Angus in 1392 and could not prevent a significant feud between local clans in 1396. By the end of the fourteenth century events such as these served further to antagonise the crown and emphasise the establishment's perception of the Highlands as bellicose savages. It seems fair to conclude that the population contraction in the wake of plague helped to accentuate the differences that were already emerging between Lowland and Highland society, though to what extent these would have been manifest had outbreaks not occurred is impossible to ascertain.

Aside from the Crown, the nobility and the peasantry, the Black Death also could not have failed to have had an impact on one final, extremely dominant, area of society: the Church. Throughout Christendom the effect of plague on the duties, personage and perceived infallibility of the Church was appalling – and on an unprecedented scale – and the subsequent repercussions this had for the rest of society were to be one of the most significant and most bemoaned consequences of the outbreak. Fourteenth-century Scots were monolithic in their basic faith, belonging to the international Catholic Church. They were ministered to by 3,000-4,000 churchmen organised hierarchically, with the figurehead of the Pope as important in the political arena as the spiritual realm. The constant contact maintained with the papal Curia in Rome reflected the papacy's intense involvement in non-spiritual matters: of 180 known papal letters sent to Scotland before 1198, only three were even vaguely connected with belief and, of the correspondence sent during the pontificate of Clement VII (1378-94), none was. Since the late twelfth century Scotland had enjoyed a unique relationship with the papacy, immediately subject to it after having being declared a 'special daughter' in 1192 (though the dioceses of Galloway and the Isles were officially in the archbishoprics of York and Trondheim respectively) and the nation did not possess its own archbishop until 1472.

The administrative structure under which the Church was organised was a sophisticated one, with a variety of courts, councils and visitations overseeing both practical and spiritual business. The country had over 1,000 parishes grouped into a dozen dioceses, with cathedrals overseen by a bishop, dean and chapter, collectively termed the secular clergy. There were also religious houses 'staffed' by regular clergy (monks, friars and nuns) – by the early fourteenth century these comprised thirty abbeys, twenty-seven priories, twenty friaries and nine nunneries. These were owned by numerous orders, including Benedictines, Cistercians, Tironensians, Premonstratensians, Augustinians, Cluniacs, Valliscaulians, Carmelites, Dominicans and Trinitarians, all of whose establishment in Scotland between the late eleventh and late thirteenth century had largely been facilitated by secular patronage. While some of these orders drew an income (often substantial) from lands, flocks and mills, others were mendicant and chose to settle within burghs in order to beg for alms in view of their voluntary vow of absolute poverty which prevented them owning property. Whether through giving alms or the grander gesture of bestowing lands and constructing buildings, the provision of generous charity was an important act for the medieval benefactor: the seven corporal works of mercy included such charitable acts as feeding the hungry, giving drink to the thirsty and clothing the naked, each of which eased the path to Heaven through the prayers on their behalf of those whom they had chosen to endow. Conspicuous displays of piety were made both by kings, notably David I (1124-53), who founded the abbeys of Kelso (1128, Tironensian), Melrose (1136, Cistercian), Jedburgh (1138, Augustinian) and Dryburgh (1150, Pre-monstratensian), and by major landowners, such as Dervorguilla Balliol, who founded Sweetheart Abbey (1273, Cistercian). Aside from the granting of lands to cathedrals and monasteries they installed clerics as nominal rectors of parishes, thereby entitling the incumbent to the teinds (English tithes) from the parish's inhabitants (the practice known as 'appropriation'). By the early fourteenth century grants of land were increasingly replaced by annual monetary payments. Many chaplainries (the equivalent of English chantries) for the celebration of private masses for souls specified by the donor were established in cathedrals, parish churches, private chapels (often attached to castles) and collegiate churches, which were created by the combination of several chaplainries and staffed by secular clergy. All but four of these were endowed by magnates: the creation of Lincluden in Galloway by Archibald 'the Grim', Earl of Douglas in 1389 is a fine example. To what extent plague was at all a factor in their establishment can only be guessed at, though the increasing frequency with which they were established (five in the fourteenth century and eighteen between 1400 and 1469) makes it not inconceivable that there was an increased concern for the celebration of mass in the face of the perceived omnipresence of death. Economic factors were perhaps a more obvious reason: chaplainries and collegiate churches were more cost effective, providing more masses for their patrons at considerably less cost than that incurred through the granting of land to cathedrals or monasteries. That would certainly have been an important consideration given the economic contraction during the later fourteenth century and beyond and, in that sense at least, plague was a significant factor in their foundation.

In terms of mortality due to the Black Death the clergy was probably one of the worst affected groups within European society. Aside from the close-knit conditions in which they

tended to live, this was probably a consequence of the fundamental role they played in such terrible times, as their basic
duties of ministry and comfort were never more necessary
at a time when the contemplation of the imminence of
death dominated life on such a stark and unprecedented
scale. Their visiting of the sick, administering of last rites
to the dying and providing comfort both to victims and
their inconsolable relatives were all acts that made churchmen particularly vulnerable to infection, especially given the
likelihood that it was an easily communicable viral disease.
An English monk from Tynemouth noted that 'rectors and
priests, and friars also, confessing the sick, by the hearing of
the confessions, were so infected by that contagious disease
that they died more quickly even than their penitents.' It
has been estimated that the Black Death killed about 45 per
cent of the clergy in England, which would indicate a higher
percentage than the 35 per cent of the total population that
probably died. Although we do not have comparable figures for other social groups it would appear that the clergy
within Scotland suffered greatly in terms of mortality. Walter
Bower recorded that twenty-four – about a third – of the
canons of St Andrews died in the outbreak, 'of whom all
but three were priests.' This seems inordinately high (and
startling if accurate): nevertheless, his point is important in
that it indicates that the Black Death caused the deaths of a
perceptibly large number of clerics in St Andrews and probably, therefore, also in other parishes. Certainly this was a
significant problem elsewhere – to cite just one example, in
January 1349 the Bishop of Bath and Wells wrote of how
'the contagious pestilence of the present day... has left many

parish churches in our diocese without parson or priest to care for their parishoners.'

The shortage of priests had a number of practical consequences that, though unavoidable, became the focus of much disapproval from contemporaries. Positions left vacant by the death of their incumbent were often hard to fill, not least because, as Stephen Birchington of Canterbury commented, 'beneficed parsons turned away from the care of their benefices for fear of death.' As with landlords being unable to find tenants to work the land unless for higher wages, so the same situation could occur amongst the clergy of the parish. Knighton recorded that in 1349

> there was such a shortage of priests everywhere that many churches were bereft of the divine office: of masses, matins, and vespers, of sacraments and observances. A man could scarcely retain a chaplain to serve a church for less than £10, or perhaps 10 marks, and where one might have had a chaplain for four or five marks, or two marks and his keep, with such numbers of priests as there were about before the plague, now in those times there was almost no-one to willing to take a vicarage for £20, or perhaps 20 marks.

There had been a clerical recruitment crisis in Scotland long before the advent of the Black Death. The rise of nationalism and the eruption of the civil wars both played a part in this. So did the prosperity of the thirteenth century, which had permeated the Church as much as other areas of society and thereby alienated some who sought a truly austere lifestyle.

This may be evidenced in the successful establishment of only two houses – both in Ayrshire – by the Cluniac order, whose promotion of a return to primitive austerity won few Scottish converts in the thirteenth century. Nevertheless, it may not be without significance that the one monastery founded after 1300 was that of the Carthusians, at Perth in 1429, an order renowned for its adherence to asceticism. The fact that this was the only monastic foundation after the thirteenth century demonstrates that the expansion of many orders had slowed down long before the advent of plague. It is unsurprising that the mortality caused by the Black Death must therefore have dealt a bitter blow to the already falling monastic numbers in Scotland. This was probably particularly true of the Highlands where monasticism had made fewer inroads than other parts of the country, although it must be borne in mind that the comparative paucity of sources for the area makes it hard to assess this decisively. Further south, monastic decline certainly set in by the late fourteenth century, with the suppression of, amongst others, Lincluden and Berwick nunneries c.1390. The complaint from the Cistercian monastery of Saddell in Kintyre around 1507 that there had been no monastic life there in living memory was almost certainly not untypical, while in 1462 Kelso Abbey had recruited only half its possible number of clergy. This situation needs to be balanced by indications that the decline was not irreversible: by 1540 the number of monks at Kelso had risen and there is evidence that other houses, such as Lindores, maintained recruitment levels into the sixteenth century. The arrival in Scotland of the Observant Franciscans in the later fifteenth century also attracted a healthy number of converts. Although the numbers of recruits fluctuated after the 'golden age' of medieval monasticism in the thirteenth century, they nevertheless remained sufficient to ensure that nunneries, monasteries, churches and collegiate chapels were a major part of the landscape of fourteenth-century Scotland and their endowment and continued patronage an important – indeed, ostentatious – act of piety for the nation's wealthier inhabitants.

Across Europe attempts were made in two ways to surmount the critical shortage of clergy in the wake of the Black Death. The first was through the appointment of replacements unskilled for the job. As Knighton complained, 'within a short time there came into holy orders a great multitude of those whose wives had died in the plague, many of them illiterate, the merest laymen, who if they were able to read at all were unable to understand what they read.' Despite the grumbling of chroniclers, in practice a university education was not a prerequisite of ecclesiastical work. Clerics were offered teaching by their ecclesiastical superiors, in the diocese of St Andrews, at least, where instruction was proposed in the sacraments and other necessary matters. Similarly, there is a lot to be said for the argument that experience is the best teacher and many clerics simply learned 'on the job' by assisting other priests as a sort of apprenticeship. Having said that, education was nevertheless considered important for much of the clergy in Scotland as elsewhere, with the reading and recitation of Latin a much-promoted aspect of their work and the equally valuable skill of writing reflected in the words 'clerk' and 'clerical'. Many senior

Scottish clergymen received at least their initial training at university and, though only around 300 of the country's 1,000 parishes had graduate incumbents, this was proportionately similar to the rest of Western Christendom. Before the foundation of St Andrews University in 1412, Scots seeking an education had to journey elsewhere, perhaps south to Oxford or (more rarely) Cambridge, or especially with the onset of the Anglo-Scottish wars, to one of the great continental institutions such as Paris or Bologna. This necessarily gave Scottish graduates a cosmopolitan outlook and ensured their integration with, and valuable contribution to, European intellectual life and theory. It also meant the infiltration into Scotland of numerous and varied textbooks which found their way into monastic and cathedral libraries throughout the country. By 1436 that of Aberdeen cathedral was not alone in boasting works on many theological and philosophical subjects, including texts of Augustus, Aquinas and Isidore.

No Scottish chronicler complained about the installation of unqualified clerical incumbents in the wake of the Black Death although, if Bower's evidence is to be accepted, then this cannot have been because the clergy were not badly affected by plague. Rather more likely was the paradoxical fact that the proportion of educated clergy at the highest level actually rose after the Black Death, with at least four-fifths of episcopal appointments between 1350 and 1425 going to university men. It was perhaps only in Galloway that non-graduates were more commonly installed, while the evidence for the Highlands is too complicated to draw firm conclusions. This was a higher proportion than in England

'Der Pfarrherr', *the Parish Priest by Holbein: as men of God it was the role of the parish preist to comfort the sick and perform last rites, a duty which became of utmost importance during the Black Death. The significance of this contributed to their being one of the worst affected groups in terms of mortality*

(fewer than 70 per cent of Edward III's bishops were graduates), which may help to explain why Knighton asserted that the standard of education had fallen after the plague whereas Scottish chroniclers did not. Of course, the fact that more bishops were educated would not have made much noticeable difference to the vast majority of parishioners, who most likely had very little (if any) contact with their local bishop and simply took no interest so long as they felt that the quality of ministry remained adequate. This was probably the case, as the number of those gaining an education was also on the increase among those in monastic orders who undertook preaching to a greater extent than did the secular clergy. During the later fourteenth century at least twelve houses arranged for some of their members to go to university to study theology or canon law, whereas few appeared to have undertaken any such education earlier in the century. This meant that, in the words of Donald Watt, 'the intellectual level of at least some of the Scottish monasteries rose appreciably towards the end of [the fourteenth century].' Interestingly, this was particularly true of St Andrews, largely as a result of the encouragement of the Augustinian prior of the cathedral, James Bisset. This may help to explain why Walter Bower, writing in the 1440s, lamented the numbers of canons dying in the parish but not the subsequent installation of uneducated replacements, which was apparently so frequently the case in England and elsewhere.

The other way in which vacated benefices could be filled in the wake of the Black Death was through pluralism – the acquisition of extra ecclesiastical offices and, with it, the attached salary and other benefits. Elsewhere it was a common practice noted by many observers. In one area of Germany thirty-nine benefices were held by thirteen men in the period 1345-47: by 1350-52 this had become fifty-seven offices in the hands of only twelve. The example is far from extreme. The financial benefits of multiple occupancy ensured that pluralism was already endemic among archdeacons, deans and canons in Scotland by the time of plague. To cite one example, William Wishart, Bishop of Glasgow, in the late thirteenth century had allegedly amassed twenty-two rectories and prebends by the time of his election. Pluralism remained common among archdeacons, deans and canons after the Black Death, which is unsurprising considering Bower's evidence of such high mortality rates among the canons in St Andrews. The financial incentive was as important as the practical need to fill offices, for plague badly affected the Church's economic fortunes. As with secular lands the value of rents fell – in the 1366 revision of land values those of the Church depreciated by 37 per cent. This particularly affected the regular clergy (for whom pluralism was not an option), as they were among the largest landowners. The demand for wool would have brought temporary relief for those abbeys, such as Melrose, which owned large flocks of sheep and the effects of inflation were first felt only in the 1390s. Efficient land management, such as that evidenced by Coupar Angus Abbey, also helped somewhat though still not enough to return land values to their thirteenth-century levels. The changing pattern of endowments in the aftermath of plague hurt the secular clergy badly, as patrons' poor finances after plague led them to invest more in cost-effective collegiate churches. Bower's comment, that Bishop Wardlaw of St Andrews (1403-40) 'entertained daily with a lavishness beyond his means', indicates financial pressure in the country's richest see and from the early fifteenth century instances of pluralism became more commonly recorded. Poverty, among the lesser clergy at least, had long been common. In the thirteenth century vicars who earned a fixed pension were supposed to receive ten merks and chaplains £5. By the fourteenth century such vicars were supposed to be paid £10, putting them on a par with many substantial husbandmen. In reality, however, many were not. Plague, however, merely exacerbated an existing trend. The fact that Scottish chroniclers did not complain about pluralism perhaps suggests that the practice was not noticeably more prolific after the Black Death than it had been before. As with the rest of society, the economic effects of plague on the Church may not have been so terrible as elsewhere because the outbreak was less severe.

Whether offices remained unoccupied or were filled by inappropriate appointments, the shortage of skilled priests entailed serious neglect of essential duties. Beginning at birth with the act of baptism it was the job of church personnel, as God's representatives on earth, to administer the sacraments necessary for the salvation of their parishioners and, to do so, in the words of thirteenth-century Scottish Church statutes, 'with devout solemnity in the Catholic faith according to the precise form handed down by the holy fathers and the holy scriptures.' These sacraments included communion at mass (the celebration of the Eucharist, which commemorates Christ's passion). Bower dedicated a chapter of his chronicle to the merits of this ceremony, describing it as 'the salvation of the living and the redemption of the dead.' Also important was the receiving of absolution after confession and penance (which demonstrated genuine repentance); the performing of these last rites at the time of death was particularly important. They were considered vital for the avoidance of eternal damnation and the lessening of the time to be spent in purgatory, which was a period of punishment after death required by God for the complete expiation of guilt. For every member of the Catholic Church the exact length of time this would last was dictated both by the earthly actions of the individual and by the act of confession and receiving of absolution before death. A 'good death' was deemed vital and handbooks on the craft of dying were commonly studied in order to teach the preparations necessary for the inevitable afterlife. Dying unprepared without having confessed and been absolved from sin was a major fear of the medieval Christian and one that the imminence of death must have heightened considerably. The onset of plague was therefore doubly terrifying: aside from the horrific suffering the disease inflicted on victims in the present life, there was also possibility of it killing them before absolution could be granted – 'that we sowld thus be haistely put down, and dye as beistis without confessioun' was how Robert Henryson described it in the fifteenth-century 'Ane Prayer for the Pest'. The sentiment was felt equally in the fourteenth century: at Bannockburn in 1314 the Scots apparently knelt in prayer before attacking, no doubt in anticipation of death.

The shortage of clergy to carry out these vital last rites was therefore considered a serious problem during the Black Death. In January 1349 the Bishop of Bath and Wells advised that, given the lack of priests, parishioners should ensure that if 'on the point of death… [they were to] make confession… even to a woman': this course of action was theologically acceptable but never normally recommended by the Church.

If two-thirds of the St Andrews canons had indeed died, then we can assume that this must have been a common practice in that see, though there is no surviving evidence that the shortage necessitated any plea similar to that made by the Archbishop of York. His request for an emergency ordination of new priests to help meet demand was granted by Clement VI in November 1349. Under pressure from many countries that had an acute shortage of clerics, the Pope declared 1350 a Jubilee year during which those who travelled to Rome would be granted a plenary indulgence, ensuring release from other penances due to be undertaken as a result of sins already committed. Participants travelled there from all over Christendom (although Knighton recorded that English pilgrims wishing to travel were initially prevented from doing so by the king 'because of the war with France'). The Italian observer Matteo Villani reckoned there must have been more than a million visitors that year. Despite (or perhaps because of) the outbreak of the Black Death, the abbot of Dunfermline undertook the journey, according to Bower, and we may assume he was not alone among his fellow Scots.

The shortage of clergy entailed that the Church neglected society's spiritual care. While the phenomenon was not apparent in Scotland, elsewhere acts of violence were perpetuated against the clergy by some who felt let down and abandoned. In England reports of such incidents became more frequent during the Black Death: to cite one example, the prior of St Mary was chased by a crowd brandishing 'bows and arrows and other offensive weapons', who also tried to set fire to the buildings. Rather than genuinely blaming the clergy, it is probable that the locals merely wished to take their horror and frustration out on someone and the Church, so pervasive in society, seemed an easy target, especially given its failure to warn its flocks of the plague or protect them once infection broke out. This could be taken a stage further to what some contemporary observers believed to be a logical conclusion: the attribution of the Black Death's arrival to clerical immorality. By the end of the thirteenth century, the Church as an institution had been accused of becoming increasingly preoccupied with secular affairs, the clergy involving themselves in politics in order to increase their own power and becoming less concerned with performing their pastoral duties. Many contemporary chronicles provide the overwhelming impression that the clergy were utterly corrupt, sinful, selfish, greedy and wholly unfit to represent God on earth. However, relying solely on their evidence would be completely misleading – commentators were bound to record examples of such shocking behaviour. For that is precisely what they were: unusual and therefore newsworthy. There was no interest in recording the everyday exploits of the vast majority of clerics whom we may presume struggled hard to carry out their proscribed duties faithfully. Assuming chroniclers' accounts to be an accurate representation of the medieval Church is akin to future generations judging the entire medical profession on the basis of what they read in today's newspapers, which only report the rare instances of professional neglect or abuse. In the aftermath of plague and other disasters it was easy for commentators to use the benefit of hindsight to regard such events as the logical outcome of such untoward behaviour.

Thus the Black Death came to be seen by some as divine revenge for the faults of the clergy. An anonymous poet lamented that:

> England mourns, drenched in tears. The people, stained with sin, quaked with grief. Why? Because… the priests of God are unchaste; their deeds not matching their name. They should be teaching and administering the sacraments, but they behave in ways inappropriate to their order.

No Scottish chronicler specifically attributed the arrival of plague in 1350 to clerical immorality: indeed, the St Andrews canons who died from the disease were described by Bower as 'men of ample education, circumspect in spiritual and in temporal matters, and upright and honourable in their way of life.' The nation's clerics were not faultless, however. Breaches of the rule of clerical chastity were by no means uncommon, as were (in spite of Bower's description) the numerous misdeeds recorded in the late fourteenth-century diocesan statutes from St Andrews: churchmen were found carrying weapons (forbidden except when embarking on journeys, when long knives were permitted); engaging in dancing, wrestling and unseemly sports (which could be bloody as well as immoral); having concubines; and celebrating extra masses purely for financial gain. But neither should these records be regarded as accurate, as once again the clergy they described were considered noteworthy exceptions. Moreover, efforts were made – notably at Iona in 1426 – to rid the profession of those whose immorality brought complaints. For want

'Vßtribung Ade Eue', *the expulsion*

of a more decisive and obvious explanation, the apparent absence of dissatisfaction with the clergy either on the part of chroniclers or congregations in the wake of the Black Death could perhaps be attributed to the overall limited effect the epidemic had on the nation.

The Black Death has been credited with instigating – though more properly this should rather be accelerating – intellectual scepticism of the Church, regarding both its personnel and its theology. Despite the material and mortal damage the Black Death inflicted upon the Church, the impact plague had on its infallibility as an institution arguably had far greater consequences in the long term. In the opinion of critics the clergy's inability to provide sufficient comfort and support at a time when it was most required was compounded by the Church's teaching that society had collectively brought the disaster of plague upon itself. The imminence of death and the afterlife coupled with the earthly horror that was everywhere apparent, therefore paradoxically called into question the one unshakeable aspect of medieval life: faith. The interpretation of plague as ultimately a divine punishment fundamentally directed both medical and spiritual responses to the Black Death throughout Christendom and it is to these that we now turn.

3

The Responses to
the Black Death in Scotland

he coming of the Black Death in their midst caused Europeans to advance all sorts of explanations for its initial arrival, its spread and the widespread devastation it caused. In the absence of satisfactory medical identification, society had no awareness of the clinical nature of the disease, a situation which seemed to emphasise the terrifyingly indiscriminate way in which it attacked communities, localities and countries. Numerous immediate causes were blamed for the outbreak of plague: aside from the lax morals of the clergy, disobedient children and inappropriately dressed men were also believed to be among the many likely culprits. Each of these was a secondary cause that had one essential element in common: they all incurred God's displeasure. Whatever myriad explanations were offered for plague (and however many correlating cures) medieval society understood one crucial, fundamental fact about the pandemic: it was wrought upon them by God, who wished to punish sin and immorality. In the East this was interpreted as being carried out on an individual basis, with God striking particular people for certain sinful acts. As He had purposefully chosen sufferers, plague was therefore seen as a blessing, to be celebrated as a sign of God's special treatment. In Western Christendom, on the other hand, plague was interpreted as being inflicted upon society as a whole for its collective sins.

The recognition by physicians and chroniclers alike of this disturbing fact and all that it implied, provided society not only with an interpretive framework for the causes of plague, but also an obvious solution for avoiding, limiting and curing the disease. This attitude fundamentally informed responses to the Black Death on every level, from the individual who strived feverishly to appease God in whichever way necessary, to the learned physicians of the day whose unshakable knowledge of the ultimate cause did not preclude belief in numerous secondary causes which equally required addressing.

The Black Death was not the first epidemic Western Christendom had confronted and the learned thinkers of the day were widely aware of the course of the First Pandemic, which had swept across Europe in the sixth century. Through the philosophical works of classical writers they were further provided with descriptions of plague, as well as its origins, causes and cures. Likewise, medieval man did not need to look far to find antecedents, for they were plainly spoken of in the Bible providing him with an explanation for the onset of such a devastating outbreak. The message was immediately clear: God had sent the plague as a vengeful punishment for sin, just as He had done to the people of Egypt and Israel for their disobedient, immoral actions. While John of Fordun pronounced plague to have 'never been heard of by man, nor [to have been] found in books, for the enlightenment of those who come after', he may have reasoned that this was because Scotland had apparently avoided the First Pandemic altogether. In any case, he was aware that the epidemic had been caused by sin, as he noted that Scots at the time were nevertheless sinful. Likewise, Bower noted that 'these plagues occur from time to time because of the sins of mankind.' Knighton acknowledged overtly that Scots recognised sin as the cause of the mid-fourteenth century outbreak, noting that they saw it afflicting their English enemies and 'attributed it to the avenging hand of God.' This most likely provided a sense of justification given that Anglo-Scottish hostilities were then so acute. To the medieval mind it naturally followed that the way to avoid pestilence was by remedying that which angered God in the first place: indeed, the Bible had clearly signalled that repentance was the only way to ensure respite.

This primarily necessitated prayer. In order to seek forgiveness for collective sin (and thereby avoid infection from plague) it was necessary to appeal to God for mercy. However, it was not considered proper to undertake this course of action directly oneself. Instead, the preferred intercessors were the clergy, as they were regarded as being closer to God and more able to win favour. The clergy, however, was one social group to suffer greatly when the epidemic broke out, ensuring (as the previous chapter showed) that in many places (including Scotland) fewer survived who were able to perform their duties. As a substitute – and equally as a first choice – the most obvious course of action was to turn to the saints for help. As intercessors between God and man, saints were central to medieval piety. As such, they were probably more accessible than God Himself: after all, they themselves had once been human. When the Black Death initially appeared many people in western Christendom turned to three saints in particular for help. St Sebastian had long been invoked to help fight disease and his traditional healing properties now became of even greater significance. This was partly a result of his martyrdom – he was ordered to be executed by arrows for refusing, as a Roman soldier, to worship the Imperial cult, but was cured by St Irene. As a result he was portrayed as being pierced with arrows all over his body. This was interpreted as significant in times of plague on two levels. Firstly, the appearance of his wounds as bloody holes where he had been pierced resembled the black swellings that characterised many manifestations of the Black Death. Secondly, the epidemic was frequently likened to an attack by arrows: many of them were fired and while some people were hit and struck down others escaped altogether. As the mother of God, Mary was another extremely popular saint, with devotional prayers such as *Ave Maria* expected to be recited frequently by all Christians in Scotland as else-where. Though many representations of her were destroyed at the time of the Reformation in the sixteenth century, a number of statues and paintings survive to suggest that images of her were prolific in Scottish churches. They were also common on seals, secular as well as ecclesiastical, as that of the royal chamberlain Walter Biggar from the mid-fourteenth century shows. Mary became all the more popular with the outbreak of plague and she was commonly called upon to 'be our shield from stroke of pestilence', as an English prayer implored. Like Sebastian, she was often portrayed elsewhere in Europe as shielding souls from an onslaught of arrows. St Roche also became particularly associated with plague, most notably because he had dedicated his life to care of the sick. While his death in 1327 makes it unlikely that he died from

rogantes ut ad accipiendã benedictionẽ ad
se hc afferri pmitteret. Quẽ cũ ad se pductũ
acerrime uexatũ ĉspiceret: iussit oms secẽ
dere longi. Et ad solita oratõis arma ĉfu
gien: data benedictione pepulit peste. quã
sollicita medicoꝝ manꝰ pigmtoꝝ cõpositiõe
nequerat. Demq; eadẽ hora surgens. & accep
to cibo ĉfortat: reddita dõ grarũ actione re
gressuse. ad eas que se portauerant feminas.
Sicq; factũ e: utque eũ illo tristes languidũ
aduexerant: cũ eis inde gaudentib; & ipse
sospes ac letabundꝰ domũ redirec. xxxiii.
Qm tpr mortalitatı morienté puerũ matri
sanũ restituerit.

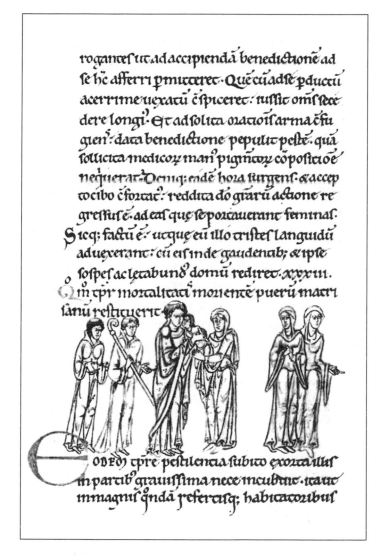

EODẼ tpre pestilencia subito exorta illis
in partib; grauissima nece incubuic. itaut
in magnis ꝗ̃ndã refercisq; habitatoribus

St Cuthbert's cure of a child dying from plague

plague, as has often been asserted, he did have a wound on his thigh that looked remarkably like a bubo. This too was reflected in his iconography, as he was often shown pointing to this swollen wound.

Scots certainly believed in the importance of saints, including those commonly invoked elsewhere. The *Book of Pluscarden*, written only slightly later than the outbreak, noted that 'the sovereign remedy for plague is to pay vows to St Sebastian, as appears more clearly in the legend of his life.' Bower also acknowledged the importance of Sebastian, recording that an earlier outbreak of plague had ceased in Rome after the citizens built an altar dedicated to that saint. One saint who had associations both with Scotland and plague was Cuthbert, previously Bishop of Lindisfarne, who was born near Melrose around AD 635. He was said to have been struck by plague in AD 661 but to have recovered, and became credited with many instances of miraculous cures. There is no evidence, however, that he was particularly invoked with the outbreak of the Black Death. Instead, when Scottish soldiers first heard of the plague decimating the garrisons of their English enemies, a common prayer became uttered:

> God and Sen Mungo, Sen Ninian and Seynt Andrew
> scheld us this day and ilka [every] day fro Goddis grace
> and the foule deth that Ynglessh men dyene upon.

Why might the Scots have chosen to invoke Andrew, Ninian and Mungo in particular? It is worth briefly summarising the lives of each. Andrew, one of the Apostles, was Scotland's patron saint, though was far from uniquely Scottish, being popular also in Burgundy and elsewhere, including Russia, of which he is also patron saint. Ninian was born in Galloway and it was he who brought Christianity to Scotland at the end of the fourth century, arriving at Whithorn and founding the priory there in AD 397. He had his famous followers – Robert Bruce was said to have particularly venerated him and the future Edward II of England visited his shrine at Whithorn in 1301. Mungo (meaning 'dear one') was originally named Kentigern and was possibly born in Fife. Consecrated as Bishop in AD 540, he undertook much preaching and missionary work and built up a following which became known as *Clasgu* (meaning 'dear family'). This group grew into modern-day Glasgow, of which Mungo is the patron saint. He died there in AD 603. He was for a time a hermit in Bewcastle, where a fine seventh-century carved stone cross survives depicting Christ in majesty and John the Baptist.

It is not without significance that Ninian and Mungo were saints who both had particular local associations with southern Scotland and is certainly noticeable that each had very strong ties with the nation in some form. Under the circumstances, the comfort each was immediately deemed to provide should not be regarded as too surprising: after all, the forces invoking them were then currently engaged in a stand-off with their English enemies, who threatened the very independence of their nation. Little wonder, perhaps, that such particularly Scottish saints should immediately be invoked. In the absence of any other explanation, it seems plausible that the Scots' choice of saints to ward off the Black Death had little to do with plague and everything to do with an assertion of nationalism. However, it is important to keep this in perspective. During the thirteenth and fourteenth centuries, religious cults in Scotland were peculiarly cosmopolitan, due in no small measure to the standard adoption of English liturgical practice, despite the outbreak of Anglo-Scottish war. This certainly holds true with regard to those Scottish hospitals founded between the mid-thirteenth and end of the fourteenth century, with the three most common dedications being to Mary Magdalene, John the Baptist and Leonard. In the period when the Black Death struck, the amalgam of international, national and local saints, so common in much of Christendom, was generally less evident in Scotland. Only with regard to plague was this later trend immediately apparent, with Scots turning in the first instance to saints of local and national importance, as well as to those associated internationally with plague. Among contemporary Scottish chroniclers the author of the *Book of Pluscarden* was apparently alone in his explicit veneration of Sebastian when the Black Death arrived. While ordinary Scots may well have invoked specific plague saints, it was only during later outbreaks that the cults of Sebastian and Roche made a particular impact. By the early sixteenth century, chapels were dedicated to each in burghs nationwide, including Edinburgh, Glasgow, Stirling, Aberdeen and Dundee.

Fourteenth-century popular expressions of faith were manifested in various ways. It has already been noted that there was a belief among Scots that the Black Death was divine retribution for society's sins; likewise there was a belief in the perceived fundamental importance of saints as intercessors between man and God. Beyond the comments of chroniclers, less evidence survives for the precise way in which this was expressed among ordinary society. A number of individual instances are apparent: we know the Abbot of Dunfermline travelled to Rome in 1350 to receive the plenary indulgence offered by Clement VI; we know also that Scottish soldiers reportedly prayed to various local and national saints when they first heard of plague's imminence; we also know that the author of the *Book of Pluscarden* believed in the necessity of appealing to St Sebastian. But what of the ordinary man? The peasant in the field, the baker in the burgh? As is regrettably so often the case in history, the voices of the majority often go unrecorded. In the absence of decisive evidence it is necessary to make some general assumptions based on the evidence that does survive.

One aspect of faith that is clear is that being near to the saints, either literally or spiritually, was both important and beneficial. Hence cults of saints and of their relics were popular manifestations of medieval piety. Evidence survives to indicate that the collecting of relics, parts of the saint's body or other artefacts closely related to him or her, was an important part of devotional practice in fourteenth-century Scotland. Relics came not only from Scottish saints but also from further afield, including a number brought back by crusaders returning from the Holy Land. Coldingham Priory possessed the bones of Saints Ebba and Margaret before 1379, at which time they were allegedly stolen and removed to Durham by the English prior William Claxton. Relics of particular saints associated internationally with plague are not known to have existed in Scotland in the aftermath of the Black Death, though this situation later changed. In 1502, when plague was again sweeping the country, King James IV paid fifteen French crowns for a bone of St Roche. Pilgrimage to visit these relics enabled the devout believer to be nearer that particular saint and thereby benefit more from their miraculous power, especially if one could touch the relic in question. This was considered especially important at a time of crisis, when the intervention of a saint was sought to alleviate a particular problem, or was undertaken in order to give thanks for prayers for intercession that had been answered. It could also be a journey embarked upon, either voluntarily or enforced, in order to receive penance for sins. Pilgrimage shrines were scattered throughout Europe. They largely attracted a local clientele, but those of the more renowned saints drew visitors from far and wide, many of whom might have journeyed for weeks. An important pilgrimage site in Scotland was that of St Ninian, whose shrine at Whithorn was where he had first landed. While he was apparently invoked at the time of the Black Death, we have no evidence of a rise in visitors to his shrine during 1350. Scotland could boast few sites of international renown, though veneration of St Margaret attracted English forces to Dunfermline in 1334 and, during the fourteenth century, the town of St Andrews was the third most common destination for pilgrims from Ypres seeking expiation from various crimes. The pilgrimage traffic also flowed in the opposite direction, with Scots, between the mid-thirteenth and mid-sixteenth centuries, frequently making the journey to one of the major pilgrimage centres in either the

East or the West. Scots travelled to the East to visit holy sites at Jerusalem and Bethlehem: one hardy Scot, Alan de Wyntoun, journeyed further across the Sinai desert to the shrine of St Catherine in 1347. In the West the major centres of pilgrimage were Rome, the seat of the papacy during most of the period, and Compostella in Spain, which apparently attracted a small but steady stream of Scots throughout the Middle Ages. The reasons for visiting particular shrines varied according to the individual, from those who venerated saints with a family or trade association, to those already in the vicinity whilst on business and those who sought out certain saints for the particular help they offered. The major pilgrimage sites were some distance from Scotland, so the willingness of Scots to travel great distances perhaps lends testimony to their devotion and their devout veneration of a cosmopolitan range of saints.

The limited propagation of a cult of 'national' saints has been attributed to the absence of a specific Scottish Use in church services, as ecclesiastical authorities were largely able to dictate saints' popularity by choosing which of their feast days were to be observed in each church. With churchmen at this time educated in England or abroad, this is not too surprising. The clergy disseminated the faith to society, ensuring that the tenets of Christianity were as important to every inhabitant of fourteenth-century Scotland as elsewhere. Each had a fundamental belief in the realities of sin, purgatory, heaven and hell, though it is improbable that their understanding extended much beyond these essentials. Church services were conducted in Latin making it unlikely that the congregation would actually be able to understand what was being said, hence the importance of iconography. Preaching undertaken in the vernacular would have been of greater benefit and incentives could be offered for listening intently to such sermons. In 1345 Scots who attended those of Roger of Lancaster, a Cistercian monk from Furness Abbey, were

Figura Mortis: *images of death became increasingly popular, especially as they reminded a non-literate society of the immediacy of death*

granted a remission of forty days in purgatory. In practice preaching tended to be more the preserve of the various monastic orders (the order of Observant Franciscans was brought to Scotland around 1463 with the explicit aim of ministry) and the clergy concentrated on administering the sacraments necessary for the salvation of the parishioners. The congregation would have had little understanding of the theological reasoning behind rituals such as the elevation of the Host at Communion but such spectacles must, nevertheless, have appeared impressive and awe-inspiring. Similarly, the use of visual media was extremely effective in transmitting the tenets of medieval Christian faith to a non-literate society and it was common to have plays recreating and murals retelling Biblical events. These served to instil in their audience the omnipotent power of God, the importance of the saints and the necessity of a pious existence in preparation for the afterlife. Plague heightened the omnipresence of death and later medieval society's concern with mortality and the afterlife became increasingly reflected both in literature and in art throughout Europe. Death, especially in the aftermath of plague, had a similar cultural impact on Scotland.

That this was not immediately apparent in the wake of the Black Death in 1350 may be a reflection on the absence of surviving sources. For the fifteenth century there is much more evidence to demonstrate the morbid fascination with death and the afterlife, while there is nothing to suggest that such concerns had not been present during the fourteenth century as well. While Protestant reformers destroyed much religious art and architecture in the sixteenth century,

Scotland, nevertheless, still boasts some fine examples of cultural manifestations of death and the afterlife. While grave-stones from the fourteenth century (and earlier) were deco-rated simply, later examples reflect an increasing focus on the imminence and personification of death. Perhaps the most striking manifestation of this was the Dance of Death, a cultural phenomenon which embodied the medieval awareness of the omnipresence of death. It was a common motif throughout Europe even before the Black Death broke out, though it is reasonable to believe that the epidemic led to an increase in its popularity not least because it was one way of coping with the magnitude of plague. Essentially, it may be characterised as an artistic depiction of death and life, symbolised by the respec-tive presence of a skeleton and a human being. The Dance was a symbolic portrayal of the moment of death that sought to emphasise the visual opposition of the appearance of the living and the dead. It was also seen as a literal warning of the imminence of death. Those living were arranged in order of precedence within each 'vocation', hence pope, cardinal and bishop corresponded to emperor, king and duke. The skel-eton or corpse representing death danced mockingly, scorning man's earthly struggle for status and wealth at the expense of a concern for the afterlife. After all, such worldly trappings count for nothing at the time of death. The Dance was to be found throughout Europe, though it predominated in France and Germany, and was depicted in various media designed to be particularly effective in non-literate medieval society. It could physically be re-enacted as a liturgical play to illustrate ser-mons but more commonly appeared in written manuscripts, or painted on, or carved into, church walls.

Only two painted Dance of Death murals survive in Britain, both in England: a painted wooden panel at Hexham Priory in Northumberland and a painting on a stone screen in the parish church of Newark-upon-Trent. Unique amongst the representations in Britain, and the earliest that can be dated, are the stone carvings in Rosslyn Chapel, near Edinburgh, one of the best medieval examples of the Dance of Death phenomenon. The chapel was founded in 1446 by Sir William St Clair and was to be the collegiate chapel of St Mathew. The interior of the chapel is adorned with a wealth of intricate stone carvings depicting various liturgical scenes including the Fall, the seven deadly sins, the seven corporal works of mercy (one of which is burying the dead), the twelve Apostles and other scenes relating to the Nativity and the life of Christ. There are also a number of figures that show the medieval concern with death, which fall outside the scope of Dance of Death depictions only insofar as they ornament two columns and cannot truly be regarded as a complete series. Nevertheless, they were certainly inspired by the Dance of Death – and, at worst, are an offshoot from it. Typical of the genre and remarkably well preserved, the carving depicts a total of sixteen living figures, most of which are coupled with a skeleton. The characters represent all levels of society. The highest echelons of court and ecclesiastical life are shown as a king, a queen, a courtier (perhaps the founder, Sir William), a cardinal (with his distinctive wide hat), a bishop and a prelate. There is also a warrior with a helmet, sword and spear, an abbot and an abbess (whose wimple is visible). Females are further represented engaged in a variety of activities, including one praying, one either looking into a mirror or admiring her portrait and one seated on a chair. Everyday workers are also depicted: a ploughman with a bent back, a carpenter, a farmer and a gardener with a spade, as well as a sportsman, a child and a married couple. At least seven of these figures are accompanied by Death in the form of a skeleton, emphasising Walter Bower's lament that the indiscrimination of death made a king as likely to die as a peasant. 'Each of us', he stated, 'is born as a miserable creature amidst weeping to live in turmoil; each toils, languishes, dies and is consumed by worms to answer for his actions.' The carvings similarly impressed upon the audience that one day every human would become a skeleton after death, regardless of his station in life. They remain striking and awe-inspiring today and no doubt made an equal impression upon a fifteenth-century audience.

Although the carvings at Rosslyn post-date the Black Death, the fact that Scots were aware of the Dance of Death long before plague arrived is indicated by a curious incident recorded by several chroniclers. In 1285 Alexander III was betrothed to Yolande, daughter of the French Count of Dreux and the marriage was celebrated with a sumptuous feast in Jedburgh. Halfway through the meal, various members of the wedding party, including the groom, were astonished and not a little shocked to be privy to some sort of Dance of Death re-enactment. While it is uncertain exactly what took place, narratives make it clear that a procession was staged with Death as the lead character. Bower, with the artistic licence so frequently employed by medieval chroniclers, noted how those present found it 'difficult to decide whether it was a man or an apparition. It seemed to glide like a ghost rather than walk on feet.' The description of the Scots' reaction also makes it clear that they were not used to such an event. According to Fordun, the witnesses believed it to be a portent of doom and, while we must forgive the chronicler the benefit of hindsight, Alexander III was killed only five months later. It seems entirely plausible that those present bore witness to an early, perhaps the first, Scottish example of the Dance of Death. The bride's family probably brought the idea from France, as the Dance seemed to have originated in Paris, and arranged for the 'resplendent procession' which Fordun records took place. The details are unclear – we cannot tell whether any words were spoken or if any members of the clergy participated. Nevertheless, there seems no reason to discount the suggestion that this was a Dance of Death in an early form.

The omnipresence of death and the fundamental tenets of medieval Christianity were expressed increasingly during the fifteenth century by a number of Scottish poets. Robert Henryson's 'Ane Prayer for the Pest' specifically addressed the eventuality of plague and implored God to spare his native Dunfermline from an outbreak in the late fifteenth century. The poet's concern with the imminence of death is evident in works such as ' The Ressoning betwixt Deth and Man' and 'The Thre Deid Pollis' (skulls). 'The Morall Fabillis' and 'The Preaching of the Swallow' consider the universal truth of human weakness and its consequence and emphasises a belief in the perfection and creative goodness of God, but also the destruction and damnation of His creatures and the necessity for another, compensating world. A contemporary of Henryson's, William Dunbar, displayed a similar interest in death including the importance of that of Christ, penning poems such as 'Timor Mortis Conturbat Me', 'Surrexit Dominus de sepulchro' and 'The Passioun of Christ'. The suffering of Christ on the cross was recognised throughout Scotland in the Middle Ages, manifested in the cults of the Five Wounds, the Crown of Thorns and the Holy Blood. Altars dedicated to the Holy Blood were established by merchants in churches at Aberdeen, Dundee, Edinburgh, Perth and St Andrews. Dramatic reconstructions of Biblical stories were also staged, not only in church but also more publicly through various street processions and pageants. The play 'Ly Haliblude' was performed in Aberdeen on the feast day of Corpus Christi from 1440, with similar events also staged in Edinburgh and Perth by the fifteenth century. Thus, as integral members of medieval Christendom, Scots shared equally in the fundamental tenets of the Christian faith: whatever political or other concerns may have caused division and hostility, the concepts of heaven, hell, purgatory and sin were as real to Scots as to their English, French and German counterparts. Each retained an acute awareness that their earthly actions would be judged and would accordingly dictate God's treatment of them in the afterlife. He was equally able to control their earthly fortunes and it was unquestionably accepted that His wrath could be expressed through any number of calamities to befall society, of which the Black Death was but one. In those circumstances it became profoundly necessary to appeal for divine forgiveness in order to assuage His wrath. In so doing society had recourse to everyday expressions of faith, including pilgrimage and prayers to both God and His saints. While more evidence exists for such developments in the fifteenth century, there is absolutely no reason to suppose that a similar attitude should not have been expressed by Scots in the wake of the Black Death.

Elsewhere in Europe the belief that plague had been inflicted upon society as a result of sin initiated all sorts of explanations for its arrival in the mid-fourteenth century. The Black Death prompted contemporaries to revise events of the recent past in order to pinpoint particular causes for God's wrath. As we have already seen, this led some commentators to find significance in apparently increasing clerical immorality and in one English treatise disobedient children were also blamed for the outbreak of 1361. Further to this the recent fashion for inappropriate male attire was denounced as culpable by a monk from Westminster Abbey, who noted disdainfully that many men:

> have abandoned the old, decent style of long, full garments, for clothes which are short, tight, impractical, slashed, every part laced, strapped or buttoned up, with the sleeves of the gowns and the tippets of the hoods nagging down to absurd lengths, so that, if the truth be told, their clothes and footwear make them look more like torturers, or even demons, than men.

While each of these examples evidences disapproval, the perpetrators were not subject to wide-scale punishment. But there were human agents who were held to be specifically responsible for the spread of plague and the subsequent punishment of certain social groups – in particular the Jews – was a particularly reprehensible side effect of the Black Death. Arabs were the focus of blame in Spain, while throughout much of Europe paupers and pilgrims (of whatever nationality) were accused. However, these were ultimately considered secondary agents under the direction of all Jews and the subsequent persecution of the Jews in many parts of Europe was the most prolific and horrific manifestation of the belief in human culpability. The straightforward recitation of the numbers of those Jews persecuted in the aftermath of the Black Death for allegedly spreading plague does nothing to impress upon the modern reader the horrific suffering to which each of these innocent individuals was subjected. Most mass executions took place in Germany – the canon of Constance recorded that within a year 'all the Jews between Cologne and Austria were burnt' – though vengeful acts were also carried out in France, Italy and Switzerland. Anti-Semitism had been present in Europe for as long as Jewish communities had existed. In reality, they were the source of suspicion and resentment because they dominated the most lucrative professions, such as money lending. This had become manifested in the association of the Jew with the Antichrist and his deliberate malevolence was an image that certain sectors of authority, both secular and ecclesiastical, deliberately propagated. In 1267, for example, the Council of Vienna had forbidden the purchase of meat from Jews on the grounds that it was likely to have been poisoned while some irresponsible priests spread rumours of Jews kidnapping and torturing children. Jews represented all that was unchristian, using children's blood in religious festivals and desecrating Hosts meant for communion. In the fourteenth century

Chaucer's *Canterbury Tales* identified Jews as 'hateful to Christ and to his compaignye [company].' Jewish persecution was by no means new with the Black Death; however, the necessity of finding a scapegoat for the outbreak of plague channelled this latent distrust and hatred of Jews into particular decisive action. One simple charge was levelled against them, as noted by a contemporary German friar: 'the Jews planned to wipe out all the Christians with poison and had poisoned wells and springs everywhere. As evidence of this heinous crime, men say that bags full of poison were found in many wells and springs.' Few contemporary medical experts attempted to link the spread of plague to contaminated water supplies, still fewer believed Jews to be in any way responsible: nevertheless, the accusation by many was sufficiently accepted to instigate acts of severe and shocking vengeance in the wake of the Black Death.

The persecution of Jewish communities began within a few months of plague breaking out in Europe. Many attacks on Jews were carried out in places where infection was known to be present, while in towns where the disease had not yet arrived, the expulsion or elimination of Jews was seen as a preventative measure. Jews were burnt alive in, or removed from, Strasbourg, Frankfurt and Carcassone, to name but three cities. In the search for a scapegoat, society paid little heed to the obvious flaws in its reasoning, such as the fact that Jews were affected by plague as much as Christians. Since Jews were responsible for plague, it was presumed ridiculous to suppose that they could also suffer from it and any apparent evidence to the contrary was simply further proof of their cunning. Justification for this popular belief was found in the numerous confessions that Jews made (all of which were extracted under torture). Many authorities officially condemned the persecutions: Pope Clement VI called on Christians to exercise tolerance and restraint and those who persisted in their anti-Semitic actions were threatened with excommunication. While many government authorities authorised and instigated attacks on Jews, some actively condemned them, including the local council of Cologne and Emperor Charles IV (though the latter nevertheless took advantage of the killings by offering the Archbishop of Trier the goods of those Jews in Alsace 'who have already been killed or may still be killed'). In England few persecutions of Jews took place but this was due in no small measure to the fact that Edward I had ordered their expulsion in 1290 and their presence thereafter remained unobtrusive.

In Scotland no Jewish persecutions took place in the wake of the Black Death. It would be wrong to attribute this to complete tolerance or magnanimousness on the part of the Scots: Walter Bower certainly evidenced both anti-Semitism and anti-Islamism in his chronicle. The reason is rather more simple: fourteenth-century Scotland had no Jewish communities upon whom the frustration and fear caused by plague could be taken out, and the tiny number of Jews who may have found themselves in Scotland were sufficiently unobtrusive to incite jealousy or resentment (or at least were sufficiently few to make it into surviving records). Nevertheless, the lack of Jewish communities (and therefore of persecutions in the wake of the Black Death) also highlights the absence of another European phenomenon that, though present before the arrival of plague, was taken to new heights with the pandemic of the mid-fourteenth century.

The flagellant movement was one of the most extreme ways in which medieval Christians demonstrated their faith and, its association with anti-Semitism ensured that it proliferated in those places where Jewish persecutions took place. Both their numbers and popularity at the time of the Black Death were limited but the movement, nevertheless, merits consideration in a discussion of responses to plague through

Three-tailed scourge: this torturous instrument was used by flagellants to inflict pain on both themselves and other participants. Such acts of mutilation were undertaken as a form of penance in the hope of appeasing God and thereby curbing the spread of plague

its extremism and the revealing insight adherents offer into contemporary spiritual beliefs and practices. Flagellants had existed long before the mid-fourteenth century, but their dedication to penitence and the appeasement of God instigated a new wave of interest in them as the Black Death swept across Europe. The practice of flagellation was inspired by a belief in the necessity of atonement and characterised by the consequent extreme manifestation of this belief. For a consecutive period of thirty-three days (one for each year of Christ's earthly existence) followers journeyed from town to town in contemplative procession and performed a bizarre ritual of self-scourging in front of their captivated audiences, either in the local church or perhaps the communal market place. After stripping to the waist, each member of the group would perform collective flagellation on their own and each other's bodies. A description of their ritual was provided by the French chronicler Jean Froissart:

> …the penitents went about, coming first out of Germany. They were men who did public penance and scourged themselves with whips of hard knotted leather with little iron spikes. Some made themselves bleed very badly between the shoulder blades and some foolish women had cloths ready to catch the blood and smear it on their eyes, saying it was miraculous blood. While they were doing penance, they sang very mournful songs about nativity and the Passion of Our Lord. The object of the penance was to put a stop to the mortality, for in that time… a least a third of all the people in the world died.

Apparently the reaction of the crowd was one of near hysteria. They would accompany the ritual by chanting the Hymn of the Flagellants and, encouraged by the exhortations of the flagellants' leader, would pray to God to have mercy on society's sinners. We might well imagine how easy it would have been for the audience to have become swept up in the spectacle and to have 'quaked, sobbed and groaned in sympathy' with the pious Brethren of the Cross (as the movement was called in 1348) At its outset the flagellants were strictly regulated and well-disciplined but, with the passage of time, they began, for various reasons, to attract concern from Church leaders. The frenzied and fervent reaction of the crowds that thronged to witness their ritualistic behaviour was deemed to pose a threat to local social control. Of greater concern was the fact that flagellants were seen to be supplanting the authority of the local clergy, particularly as they began to present themselves as direct conduits to God and to offer absolution from sin, supposedly the exclusive prerogative of churchmen. The German branch of the movement, in particular, took the lead in denouncing the hierarchy of the Church, even ridiculing the administration of the sacraments that were such a fundamental expression of Catholic faith. Further to this the flagellants became a cause for concern as they evidenced increasingly messianic pretensions. Participants felt themselves to be the proclaimers of a new time, that of the preparation for the end of the world. The Black Death was interpreted by many contemporaries as an eschatological sign, heralding the imminent arrival of the Antichrist and subsequently the end of the present age. Numerous commentators discussed the plague in millenarian terms, as the Bible (particularly Revelation) supported the notion that plague was the sign that heralded the apocalypse. The perceived threat the flagellants posed to the Church, as well as their evident anti-Semitism, led Clement VI to outlaw them in October 1349. This probably explains why the movement never apparently reached Scotland: by the time plague broke out the flagellants had already received official papal condemnation and the movement waned soon thereafter.

While fundamentally acknowledging plague as being of divine origin, the belief in the deliberate culpability of human agents was generally absent from medical explanations of the Black Death. While Jacme d'Agramont, in the earliest medical treatise on the epidemic, considered it likely that one cause could have been the deliberate poisoning by 'wicked men, sons of the devil, who, by means of very false ingenuity and wicked skill, corrupt foods with various poisons and medicines', most physicians focused instead exclusively on scientific causes of plague. The spread of the epidemic across Europe prompted a swift response from the learned thinkers of the day, with at least twenty plague treatises written before 1353. To anyone who had studied the arts at a fourteenth-century European university – medical practitioners included – it was clear that any universal effect of illness had to be reduced to universal causes, according to particular unquestionable cosmological conceptions. This view came through the study of works by classical scholars, most notably Aristotle and Ptolemy, whose teachings continued to be adhered to by various Greek, Arab and Latin authorities into the late sixteenth century. John of Burgundy wrote in his plague treatise of 1365 that 'the arts of medicine and astrology balance each other, and in many respects one science supports the other in that one cannot be understood without the other.' Most of the physicians who wrote about the Black Death were compelled to establish a causal chain, which started with the universal cause of pestilence and then progressed to its particular effects. Christian natural philosophers developed the idea of a natural order which, despite being presided over by God (the supernatural, prime cause), was autonomous and – except for some exceptional cases (miracles) – was ruled by natural laws (secondary causes). These natural laws were discernable through the application of human reason and fell into two broad categories: firstly, that of remote, universal, superior and celestial causes and, secondly, that of close, particular, inferior and terrestrial causes. Crucially, the latter were absolutely dependent upon the former.

So it was that, in seeking explanations for the pestilence in the mid-fourteenth century most physicians turned equally to the movements of the stars and planets, and to other portents such as earthquakes, as to factors inherent within the environment of an infected town or region. In October 1348, at the request of King Charles VI of France, the college of the masters of the medical faculty of Paris published a *Compendium de epidimia* setting forth their collective opinion of the causes and cures for the epidemic, which had broken out in France some eight months previously. According to their calculations, the conjunction of three major planets (Saturn, Mars and Jupiter) in Aquarius on 20 March 1345 at one o'clock in the afternoon was, 'along with other conjunctions and eclipses', the remote origin of a 'deadly corruption of the surrounding air', which brought 'mortality and famine' as well as other effects. They had arrived at this conclusion through a work they attributed (erroneously) to Aristotle, according to which the conjunction of Saturn and Jupiter caused 'great mortalities and depopulation of kingdoms.' Similarly, Albertus Magnus' commentary on this work added that the conjunction of Mars and Jupiter provokes a 'great pestilence in the air, particularly when it happens in a warm and humid sign of the zodiac, as is the case now.' Jupiter was believed to elevate 'bad vapours', which were then ignited by Mars, 'an intemperately warm and dry planet' and one that the Paris masters pronounced 'wicked.'

Insofar as terrestrial causes were concerned, pestilence was believed to spread primarily through airborne vapours (known as miasma) that had been polluted by 'any particular thing which corrupts the air in substance and quality.' This should not be understood as an early version of 'air-borne' disease. Rather, miasma was more in keeping with the idea of disease by pollution. When the air became corrupted, it had an impact on those living within that air (in other words, environment): they could become ill. Plague was only one – albeit the worst – of manifold diseases that might arise from corrupted air. Furthermore, 'contagion' became frequently mentioned by contemporary commentators as a method by which plague could spread, but it is important to note that in the Middle Ages the word had a far broader meaning than is the case today and related to the spread of a specific disease by means of a whole range of methods. It could be passed interpersonally, from animals to people, or even from an inanimate object (such as cloth) to people. Crucially, contagion did not entail transmission explicitly through direct physical contact but indirect sources of infection as well. Aside from touch, some physicians also wrote of the ability to catch plague through the breath or by sight of the victim alone. An anonymous practitioner from Montpellier, writing in the spring of 1349, believed that the 'most virulent' form of plague occurred 'when the air spirit emitted from the sick person's eyes, particularly when he is dying, strikes the eye of a healthy man nearby who looks closely at him.' While contagion and miasma were considered distinct theoretical concepts, in practice they were interchangeable and hence thought equally culpable in the spread of plague. They referred to two successive stages of plague's dissemination, with the air being additionally the place where pestilence was generated.

The transmission of plague in these two ways also occurred on two levels, the general and the particular: that is, from place to place and from person to person. Agramont stressed that 'every disease that originates from pestilence in the air' was liable to be communicated from one person to another. But there was an anomaly that had to be explained: since plague was passed through a medium (the air) that was common to everyone within a given locality, why was it that not everyone succumbed to infection? Geoffrey of Meaux described how particular planetary alignments destined certain countries, cities and individuals to be worse afflicted, as, following Ptolemy, each was subject to different celestial influences and rulers 'and therefore the impact of the heavens cannot affect them all equally.' According to the planetary influence, pestilence could more easily be passed between certain people because 'transmutation is easy between bodies which have matching [celestial] qualities.' Physicians also attributed the susceptibility of an individual to his or her own particular physiological make-up. This theory stemmed from the Galenic emphasis on the determinative influence of an individual's unique humoural composition, which governed most clinical thinking. Each individual was believed to be essentially a microcosm of the universe that he inhabited; as a result, he functioned in the same way as it, being similarly influenced by external factors such as planetary movements. The universe was comprised of the four elements of fire (hot and dry), water (cold and wet), earth (cold and dry) and air (hot and wet); so the human body was made up of four corresponding humours – choler or yellow bile, phlegm or mucus, black bile and blood respectively. Good health would best be achieved by ensuring that no humour grew too powerful or too weak. An imbalance between particular humours caused corresponding illnesses and, likewise, could be remedied by certain cures appropriate to the illness in question. Agramont believed the effects of pestilence to derive from changes in the qualities of cold and heat, with the resultant production of various diseases that shared common elements. For example, overheating made cholera burn and 'dominate the remaining humours', as a result of which 'every disease generating itself from cholera' could occur. As with all illnesses, plague was primarily explained as a virulent putrefaction of the four humours, killing rapidly as the heart was suffocated by poisonous blood. As the putrefaction was internal, it had to be established by various observable outward signs, such as a change in the patient's urine or acute visible swellings. This process was necessarily case specific, as physicians sought to identify what precisely was attacking the individual body by 'seeing through' (the literal translation of diagnosis) certain observable 'signs', or 'tokens'. An appropriate cure could then be effected.

However, prevention was better than cure. In order to counter plague it was necessary to take certain steps to avoid the most likely sources of infection. This necessitated structuring your day-to-day conduct around the adequate management of six non-naturals, which had been first proposed by Aristotle. The first of these was air and environment, clearly of major importance given their role in the transmission of plague. Physicians advised an important maxim that was particularly sensible if the disease had already broken out in the locality: flee quickly and far, return slowly. Their advice was taken by those who could afford to in Scotland as elsewhere, including David II and many nobles. The relatively low death rate in Milan has been attributed to the ability of many citizens to flee to its large rural hinterland and it may also have been a factor in the relatively low number of Scottish nobles who died in the 1350 outbreak. If this course of action could not be followed, it was necessary to ensure the environment in which you remained was conducive to good health. This involved staying away from sources of putrefaction, such as 'marshy, muddy and stinking places, stagnant waters and ditches', and ventilating rooms, though care had to be taken to ensure south-facing windows were kept shut as winds from that direction were believed to carry pestilence. Unpleasant odours were to be countered by the use of rosewater and vinegar and by the burning of herbs and spices – indeed, anything aromatic – to produce sweet-smelling aromas. Other sources of pollution were to be eliminated, with advisable measures including the careful disposing of blood and other butchers' offcuts, not steeping leather in water and removing dung heaps from the streets. To any Galenist physician the link between stink and putrefaction was as obvious as that between putrefaction and pestilence.

The second category of the six non-naturals was eating and drinking. It was good to drink wine as this strengthened the body's natural heat, as well as many other prescribed foods and drinks, with moderation the general rule. The most important course of action was to avoid ingesting any substance that was too hot or spicy. Similarly, with regard to the third category (exercise and rest) physicians advised only moderate exercise. Bathing was likewise best avoided, as each of these activities 'opens the pores of the body through which the corrupted air comes into the body, and provokes a strong impression on it or on its humours.' The fourth category of non-naturals was sleep and wake, with sleep to be undertaken only in moderation. It was advisable regularly to alternate sleeping on the left and the right side of the body, in order to prevent the liver becoming overheated by the stomach. The fifth category, inanition and repletion, dealt with ensuring everything to which the body was subject was geared toward maintaining its purity. Blood-letting and enemas were advised to maintain humoural balance, while sexual relations represented a 'serious risk for the body.' The final group of non-naturals came under the heading accidents of the soul, which referred to various negative emotions that were to be avoided, including rage, sadness and solitude. Joy and delight were to be sought because 'pleasure, although it sometimes moistens the body, strengthens the spirit and the heart.' This came with the important proviso that 'no bad regime of diet, of lechery, or of other things' accidentally intermingled with it. Structuring your life around the non-naturals was believed to be your best chance of avoiding plague, allowing you to maintain your humoural balance and live your life in tempered comfort, whilst preventing infected airborne vapours entering your body through the pores of the skin.

The initial medical explanations offered for the Black Death came from continental physicians and we have no evidence for what particular action medical men within Scotland took to combat plague in the fourteenth century. At this time there certainly existed university-trained physicians and a strong tradition of monastic medicine in Scotland as well as a substantial body of medical works mostly in Latin but also in Gaelic, Norman-French or Scots. It is almost certain that, when the epidemic spread throughout the country in 1350, medical men approached its treatment in the same way as did their counterparts elsewhere. The works of classical writers such as Galen and Hippocrates were both well known and accessible to learned Scots in the fourteenth century. They were included among the core texts which formed the basis for the curriculum of every student. Before the foundation of St Andrews University in 1412 around 1,000 Scots journeyed abroad to gain an educa-

Original note of a consultation of Michael Scot at Bologna in the year 1221

tion – an average of between five and ten men a year from the mid-twelfth century onwards. They are discernible by name, though their definite origins are difficult to establish. Some of them became prolific in their chosen field, whether law, theology, the arts or medicine, and remained at foreign universities to teach. A notable theologian and scholar of international repute was John Duns Scotus, believed to have come from Duns in Berwickshire, who taught at Oxford and Paris between 1302 and 1307. In the field of medicine Michael Scot (*c.*1175- *c.*1232) was an early example. Probably hailing from the Borders, he gained a reputation whilst acting as tutor to Frederick II of Italy by composing *Liber Physionomiae*, a treatise on diseases that was partly influenced by Aristotle. He was also a practitioner of two important branches of science

– alchemy and astrology. Thomas de Duns (possibly also from the same town as Duns Scotus) taught in Paris during the 1360s, as did John Gray between 1409 and 1416. Many of these graduates returned to Scotland to find employment, whether in the government, the Church or in the service of the Crown or nobility. It is possible that prominent families, both noble and royal, employed some of those who gained a degree in medicine during the fourteenth century as their personal physicians. While David II definitely employed a foreign physician – Master Nicholas of Flanders – between 1359 and 1364, when the latter received payments totalling £21 13s 4d, the origins of other royal physicians cannot easily be discerned from their name. Robert I required a considerable amount of medical attention to treat his various ailments around the time of his death in 1329, when several payments were made to both a physician and various apothecaries (the equivalent of modern-day chemists). Two were named Jaunius and Johannus and, while his physician, Master Mavinus, lived in Perth we cannot be certain whether he originally came from Scotland. The same might be said of William, a physician practicing in Glasgow, who attended Robert III during the 1390s.

A number of Scots who definitely attended the monarchy at various times came from the MacBeth family of Highland physicians. This was but one of numerous professions that operated on a hereditary basis within the Highland clan system, with others including historians, poets and lawyers. The family of MacBeth (Beaton) grew to occupy the role of physicians to the MacDonald lordship of the Isles, after an early family member was said to have gained so great a

Charter of 1386 from King Robert II, granting Jura and neighbouring Islets to Ferchard Leche (Macbeth), the physician

reputation that he was summoned to treat Robert I where court physicians had failed. Later in the fourteenth century, Robert II employed Ferchard Leche from the same family, in return for whose services he granted land in Jura and its neighbouring Islets in 1386. The Beatons were important for the number of Gaelic medical manuscripts they produced, some of which have survived as evidence of contemporary learned beliefs, not only in Lowland Scotland but also in the supposedly 'savage' Highlands. Most of these Gaelic translations of classical medical texts date from the sixteenth century but, while the oldest which can definitely be dated comes from 1403, it is likely that several of them date from an earlier time. Some of them are translations of medical treatises from early Greek philosophers and physicians, while others are taken from texts originating from the great medical schools of Salerno and Montpellier. The margins of many contained notes added by their owners, dealing with the weather during various months and the food and drink most suitable in each.

One of the oldest can be dated to not long after 1400 and belonged to John Beaton. One of five Gaelic copies, it is a treatise on *materia medica*, including descriptions of animal, vegetable and mineral sources listed alphabetically according to their Latin, and then their Gaelic names. Each substance is described and its medicinal properties detailed, with quotations from numerous patriarchal writers including Avicenna, Galen, Hippocrates and Platearius of Salerno. One mineral to be described is the pearl, well known for its medicinal qualities and used as an antidote to plague when crushed and added to liquid concoctions:

> Margarita, i.e. a pearl. This stone is cold, dry and is found in a shell. And it grows in this way: when the shell opens it takes in its fill of poisonous dew, closes around it, and turns it into stone. The pearl that has a natural hollow in it is best, if also white. It is comforting in heart affections, and is put in electuaries. And if you wish to make the pearl white, give it to a pet pigeon to eat, and let it be left in its crop [stomach] for three or four hours. Then cut up the bird and remove the stone, and it will be pure, clear, brilliant thereafter.

Other subjects addressed in the surviving Gaelic medical manuscripts include: medical definitions; disorders including

Gaelic medical manuscript

leprosy, wounds and epilepsy; anatomy and diet; copies of
the Aphorisms of Hippocrates, the maxims of Isidore and
Bernard Gordon's *Lilium Medicinae*. Their existence proves
that medicine in the Highlands did not simply rely on 'super-
stitious' folk remedies, as is often assumed, but that learned
medical knowledge extended throughout the country. Other
physicians who practiced in Scotland during the fourteenth
century, whether of Scottish origin or not, returned from
their continental training with copies of classical texts in
Latin. While some of these existed as part of private collections (such as that belonging to Archbishop William Schevez
in the later fifteenth century), many found their way into
Scottish monastic houses, though it cannot be determined

with any certainty when these came to Scotland nor where exactly they were kept. However, it may be assumed that they provide an accurate indication of the state of medical knowledge in Scotland during the two hundred years preceding the Black Death. A twelfth- or thirteenth-century copy of the *Liber Galieni ad Glauconem* (the Book of Galen to his nephew, Glaucon) has been found to include an elaborate Celtic decoration of the capital letter, indicating that the scribe may have been of Scottish origin. The manuscript, written in Latin, was composed of two works: the first dealt with various diseases and morbid conditions, treating them under headings such as 'signs' (i.e. symptoms) and 'cures'; the second addressed the compositions of various remedial prescriptions, under headings such as 'potions' and 'ointments'. One commentary dealt with coughs, and evidenced the importance of observation in diagnosis, the necessity of balancing the humours and the danger of polluted air:

> Cough comes dry upon some, upon others moist, and accompanied by much phlegm. Upon others with want of breath and asthma, and upon others with spitting of blood or vomiting… coughs may become moist from a humour of the head… [or dry] from the diaphragm in people troubled by the stomach. In this case it may arise… from sharp-tasted food and salt diet, or from cold drink. It may also be caused by dust, smoke, or evil-smelling ground…

The sufferer was advised to 'lie up in a light and well-aired house' and ingest a concoction featuring linseed, mustard

Aphorisms of Hippocrates: 'those who escape quinsy, etc' and 'in those who are troubled by phthisis, etc' with twelfth-century commentaries seed and roasted nuts. Other medical treatises that existed in Scotland during the period included a twelfth-century commentary by Johannicus, the disciple of John of Alexandria, on the Aphorisms of Hippocrates, which were collections of works on topics concerning the workings of the human body. This extract evidences the importance of observation in diagnosis and the belief that illness arises from the putrefaction of the humours.

There also existed in fourteenth-century Scotland a miscellaneous collection, written partly in Latin and partly in Norman-French, consisting of works by various physicians (none identifiably Scottish) on medicinal recipes, doses, the practice of medicine and some astrological notes. Remedies are included to improve the vision, to check dysentery, to cure the stone and for a laxative. Another fourteenth-century manuscript contained a Latin translation of a work by the Arabic writer Serapion, which addressed simple remedies and an alphabetical index of plants, minerals and animals.

The only plague tract of Scottish origin was written by the Aberdeen physician Gilbert Skene in 1568. There is no evidence for a fourteenth-century plague commentary associated with Scotland, whether written within the country or by a Scot on the continent. It was probably the case that it took decades for specific plague literature to find its way into Scotland, which we should not consider too surprising, especially given the difficulties in disseminating literature before the advent of printing in the mid-fifteenth century. The register of Kelso monastery contained a copy of 'Ane Tretyse Agayne the Pestilens', which was a fifteenth-century translation into the Scottish vernacular of the Latin plague

Norman-French copy of recipes. This one deals with headaches tract written by John of Burgundy in 1365. The treatise describes the nature of plague, with an explanation for why buboes appeared in the armpit or groin, and the virtues of blood-letting to balance the humours:

> In man ar iij principal parts and members, the hart, the lever, and the harnys [brain], and ilk ane of thir has his clengyng plas quhar he may out his superfluites and clengs him. The hart has his clenging plas under the armys, that is in the hol of the oxster; the clenging plas of the levir is betuix the the [thigh] and the body in the holis; but the clenging plas of the harnys are under the eis [ears] or under the throte. Than this ewill comyss thus, qwen the porrys ar opyn for swm cause befor sayd, the air venoims enteyrs and alson menges the mannys blude, and sa rynnis to the hart that is gude and ruth of lyf, and distroyes the kynd of man and slayis him;…
> and than at the last within xxiiij houris, gif it be not passand out with bledyng, it festyngs in some plas, and casts a man into the agu, and maks a byl or a bolg in some part of the iij clenging plasis befor said, or else ner thaim.

John of Burgundy, therefore, believed that infected vapours entered by the pores of the skin and were carried by the blood either to the heart, the liver or the brain, the three principle bodily members which were the seats of the three souls in Greek-based natural philosophy. Each of these had a corresponding emunctory (an excretory duct): that of the heart was the armpit, of the liver was the groin and of the brain were the ears or throat. From each of these the poison could be expelled by bleeding. Phlebotomy was unanimously deemed to be beneficial, perhaps until the patient should lose consciousness, as a means of releasing the poison and halting putrefaction of the relevant member. The precise veins to be bled were determined by the observable location of damage to the body, manifested by signs such as the appearance of bodily swellings. Another commentator, the Italian Gentile da Foligno, also noted that behind the ears, the left armpit and the right groin were the usual places where 'signs' appeared to indicate malfunction of the principal members. A skilled surgeon would be able to identify and bleed the correct vein, thereby impeding the progress of the poison throughout the body. The cauterisation of buboes was also considered an effective method of drawing off the poison. For the cure of plague the treatise recommended drinking ale, white wine or vinegar mixed with water and using a powder made with various herbs and spices: the combined effects of eating and drinking these concoctions 'casts out vename fra the samyn place quhan it had entre gif a man be venomed.' Though the Scottish version dated from the fifteenth century, it is very likely, given the intellectual links between Scotland and the continent, that the knowledge of John of Burgundy's treatise had permeated the country at a much earlier date and the advice contained within would have been put into practice.

Once plague had been diagnosed, the cures that were suggested tended to be precisely the same measures as those recommended for prevention and were aimed at restoring the natural virtues in order to destroy the poisonous effects of pestilence. Physicians looked to classical authorities to prescribe various antidotes, ranging from simple foods such as garlic and vinegar, to ointments and compounds of different herbs. Pills of aloes, myrrh and saffron were popular, as were potions consisting of lemon, rosewater and peppermint. Powdered minerals could be added to these drinks, as physicians recognised the medicinal qualities of emeralds, pearls and gold. These were to be administered sometimes naturally and sometimes under the influence of certain celestial configurations. Substantial evidence survives to indicate the sort of practical treatments dispensed in Scotland during the fourteenth century. Much of this comes from the monasteries, one important source of health care for the medieval pilgrim or traveller. The hospitals attached to monastic houses performed a different function from that of modern institutions. Their main purpose was to provide sanctity and charity, though medical care was also dispensed to various clients including lepers, lunatics and the old. The important medieval hospital of Soutra was established in the mid-twelfth century by the Augustinians and its location south of Edinburgh near the monasteries of Dryburgh and Kelso, suggests that its purpose was to tend those pilgrims and others journeying to these abbeys. Deposits of blood indicate that blood-letting was a regular practice, a find substantiated by the discovery of medicinal waste in drains running from the site. This comprised fragments of linen dressings, pottery associated with pharmaceutical use, a possible scalpel blade, and various herbs and spices. These last items included a combination of seeds from three poisonous plants – black henbane, opium poppy and hemlock – and can be dated to the early fourteenth century. It is believed they survived as a result of the drains being choked due to the presence of a large occupying force, most likely that of the English shortly before the battle of Bannockburn. The seeds were most likely mixed together to make an anaesthetic to be taken before major surgery, probably amputation. The discovery of traces of quicklime indicates attempts to deodorise and disinfect wounds.

Other, more routine medical procedures were also carried out. An ointment jar was found to contain a pain-killing preparation composed of opium poppy in a base of animal grease. The fat from creatures such as deer often formed the base of ointments while opium poppy was a known narcotic and was one of the most common microscopic plant remains found at Soutra, along with hemp and flax. Ergot fungus and juniper berries dating from the fourteenth century were also unearthed, most likely used to induce uterine contractions either in childbirth or abortions. While the medicinal uses to which these plants were put are necessarily assumed, the findings at Soutra indicate the presence of an important hospital dispensing a wide range of medical treatments to patients from various walks of life. Although Soutra was unusually large and therefore probably had more *materia medica* at its disposal, religious houses throughout the country would have dispensed similar treatment. Shortly before the battle of Falkirk, in July 1298, Edward I was injured by his horse and had to be transported to Torphichen Priory to receive treatment. It is probably testimony to the skill of those priors that the king was taken some eight miles for medical aid, especially given that he already had in his retinue seven medical men of his own, including a physician, two surgeons and all their assistants. Nine years later, in 1307, the English king again required attention for his ailing health, this time at Lanercost Priory near Carlisle. Situated only some ten miles from the border, it is probable that the sort of health care offered there was the same as that available at the abbeys just over the border in Melrose, Dryburgh, Jedburgh or Kelso. Edward was bathed in aromatic herbs and flowers (at a cost of 110s) and was given a desiccative ointment of aloes and balsam, as well as a concoction containing amber, musk, pearl, gold and silver. Included in the physician's account, on the instructions of the king, were items for various men, some of whom were Scots, or at least resided in Scotland, including Peter of Coldingham, who received a quantity of non-descript syrup and medicine. The whole bill came to a substantial £134 16s 4d and indicates the availability of various medicines at least in the south of Scotland. There certainly existed both the medicines and the expertise to treat a variety of common complaints fairly easily. Likewise, so did the fourteenth-century understanding of the workings of the human body and the influence of celestial movements, and the interpretation of plague as internal putrefaction caused by a humoural imbalance and evidenced by observable signs. It was understood in Scotland as elsewhere that infection was spread by polluted airborne vapours that entered the body through the pores as well as contagion through the gaze, breath or touch of an infected person. Medical men in Scotland also appreciated the importance of avoiding the various sources of pollution: not only sufferers themselves but also wider causative agents such as foul odours and polluted water from which infection could arise.

These beliefs had implications for national parliaments and local town councils alike, as both were compelled to protect the health of the citizens they governed. With no bureaucratic framework in place for dealing with the Black Death, in its immediate wake, government responses were on an individual and reactionary basis. They did not become co-ordinated until later outbreaks began to evidence a discernible pattern and thereby necessitate a more formal response. The Italian cities led the way in the formation of bureaucratic plague policy; however, in the 1340s very few responded. Magistrates in Milan focused on the spread of the disease by contagion (in its wider, fourteenth-century sense) and reasoned that segregation of the town would hinder this through the monitoring and control of people and goods into and within, the city. Anyone who was believed to be infected was confined to their house and given food via baskets lowered on ropes. In Venice all incoming vessels were impounded for forty days (hence the term quarantine, from *quaranta* meaning forty) and the possibility of infection being transmitted from those who had died meant that all victims had to be buried at least five feet deep. Over time, a more organised and systematic approach became adopted, as local governments began to build up networks of information about the extent of the disease and liase with neighbouring towns to discuss co-ordinated responses. Specific public health boards were eventually created in many towns, principally in Italy, in order to effectively manage the huge administrative task of dealing with large-scale epidemics (and to oversee health care in general). This was both a costly and complicated venture. Plague necessitated the employment of numerous personnel:

medical practitioners to treat sufferers and advise on policy; officials to monitor people and to guard town entrances; literate scribes to maintain efficient records; messengers to liase with neighbouring towns; gravediggers and fumigators to deal with the practical effects of massive mortality. The necessity of maintaining a clean environment was also recognised and numerous efforts were made to ensure that communal water supplies were untainted by by-products from trades such as butchery and tanning, that domesticated animals such as pigs, dogs and cats were controlled and that dung-heaps were regularly removed from the main streets.

By the sixteenth century the major Scottish burghs shared in most of these organised bureaucratic responses, by implementing standard measures for limiting the movement of people and goods (with the earliest quarantine regulations being implemented in Peebles in 1468), cleansing the environment, segregating the infected, seeking out and identifying victims, targeting beggars and vagabonds and providing for sufferers. We have no record of what measures (if any) were implemented by either local or national government in Scotland in the immediate aftermath of the Black Death. However, national legislation had long been in place for dealing with sufferers of another affliction – leprosy – which indicates that the bureaucratic understanding of how disease was spread existed by the time the Black Death arrived. Leprosy remained endemic in Scotland for centuries, though the number of sufferers was small and plague increasingly replaced it as the more feared (and, overall, more prolific) disease. The leper hospital founded outside Aberdeen, for example, admitted only three recorded patients during the last three decades of its existence at the end of the sixteenth century, by which time the building had already fallen into a state of disrepair. The stigmatisation of the disease during the fifteenth century is indicated in Robert Henryson's *Testament of Cresseid*, which sought to empathise with a sufferer, lamenting the way in which a girl who was once beautiful had become ashamedly disfigured through leprosy contracted as a result of sin. She was condemned to ostracism:

> *quhair thow cummis ilk man sall fle the place;*
> *thus sall thow go begging fra hous to hous*
> *with cop and clapper lyke ane lazarous.*

There is a convincing case to be made that the majority of individuals deemed to be lepers were not actually victims of what we know today as Hansen's disease. The condition of being leprous was most likely an artificial social construct, which had pervasive connotations of immorality. The 'diagnosis' of various skin conditions as leprosy was made by clerics, who stigmatised particular individuals in line with Biblical teachings. In the words of a Parisian monastic chronicler from the twelfth century:

> ... fornicators, concubines, the incestuous, adulterers,
> the avaricious, usurers, false witnesses, perjurers... all,
> I say, such as these, who through guilt are cut off from
> God, all are judged to be leprous by the priests.

In this, leprosy differed fundamentally from plague. Plague was indiscriminate and widespread and was sent by God to punish the collective sins of society as a whole, while leprosy was a loathsome and noticeable punishment specifically inflicted on particular individuals as result of their own sin.

According to contemporary understanding, therefore, lepers posed a threat by their ability to corrupt society not only physically, but morally as well. Early bureaucratic measures enacted in Scotland for their segregation reveal striking parallels with the way in which the arrival and spread of plague would be interpreted. During the reign of David I leper hospitals were founded in Berwick, Roxburgh, Stirling and Edinburgh, being situated outside the town boundaries, with government legislation passed for their inhabitants' care and – importantly – control. They were to receive rotten flesh unable to be sold at markets or from wild beasts found dead in the royal forests. Those unable to support themselves were to receive the sum of twenty shillings to be donated by townsfolk for the sustenance of these individuals. They were not allowed to beg from door to door but were instead only to 'pas the he [high] way thruch the toune and… sit at the toune end and thar ask almous [from] furth passand men.' Lepers carried cups in which to collect alms and were equipped with clappers to warn the public of their presence. Through forcing lepers to be identifiable and restricting where they could beg, the statute clearly sought to monitor and control their movement within the burgh, emphasised by a subsequent order forbidding residents from allowing them to stay in the town except to beg. Sufferers in Glasgow in the mid-fourteenth century were required to cover their mouth with a cloth so as to limit the possibility of transmission through their foul breath. Belief in the spread of the

disease by breath and the necessity of identifying and segregating victims were essential aspects of later governmental
legislation concerning plague. Considering that such regulations were enacted for leprosy and that the appearance of
plague gradually prompted the instigation of such legislation elsewhere, it is possible that similar proactive measures
to combat plague might also have been enacted in Scotland
earlier than the surviving records tell us.

While such legislation had long been enacted to combat
leprosy, the arrival of the Black Death presented governments and medical practitioners of the fourteenth century
with an altogether tougher challenge, although to what
extent this disease was recognised as being something 'clinically new' is difficult to say. With only one exception, no
early commentators compared the epidemic to any previous pestilence. Fordun certainly believed that the appearance
of the disease was something never before experienced in
Scotland. Although Europe had been subjected to the First
Great Pandemic, plague was apparently a 'new' disease insofar
as its symptoms were known to physicians of the day only
from the descriptions by classical writers and not from recent
personal experience. What was even more shocking about
plague was its sheer virulence, for it killed indiscriminately
and in huge numbers. This was reflected in the nomencla-
ture that was applied when it first broke out. The very term
'Black Death' came into existence only during the later
sixteenth century: contemporaries instead predominantly
used the substantive *mortalitas* (mortality), either alone or
with emphatic epithets such as great, terrible, immense and
universal. Each of these reflects the literal way in which it

was interpreted – in the absence (at this early stage) of any clinical diagnosis it was seen simply as something which was catastrophic in its mortality. 'Pestilence' and 'epidemic' were further terms employed, though they were not intended to have such specific meanings as those we would use today. Rather, each reflected the origins and nature of the infection as determined by the earliest commentator on the Black Death, Jacme d'Agramont, whose treatise on the epidemic appeared in April 1348. Following the classical writer Isidore, he split the term 'pestilence' into three syllables: *pes* (= tempesta: 'storm', 'tempest'), *te* (= *temps*: 'time'), and *lencia* (= *clardat*: 'brightness', 'light'). Hence, he concluded that 'pestilence' was 'the time of the tempest caused by light from the stars.' The word 'epidemic' was similarly interpreted by the anonymous practitioner of Montpellier as coming from the Greek *epi* (= upon) and *demos* (= containing receptacle of air, according to him): 'epidemic' therefore could be translated as 'plague in the receptacle, i.e., of the air.'

In this light it becomes understandable why Scots referred to the disease that first appeared towards the end of 1349 as 'the foul death of the English.' It was simply common sense to label it in terms of what was observed – a nasty (and terrifying) unknown entity that they believed to be killing the English. The origins of a particular disease were frequently used as a nametag when no definitive clinical term could be applied: when the disease commonly assumed to be syphilis reached Scotland in the late fifteenth and early sixteenth centuries, the burgh council of Aberdeen labelled it 'the infirmitey cumm out of franche and strang partis' and 'this strangis seiknes of Nappillis', as they believed it to have originated amongst French soldiers fighting in Naples. Acknowledging the origin (whether nefarious or otherwise) of a disease in its name remains common today, Spanish influenza, Dutch elm disease and German measles being three modern examples. In the Middle Ages, at least, if the tag could be attributed to your political nemesis so much the better. Unflattering labels were commonly applied to enemies, invariably as a result of God's displeasure: for the same reason, the English were commonly reputed to have tails, a joke circulated not only amongst Scots but Castilians, Germans and French as well. Besides this, perhaps it was somehow fitting that so devastating a disaster as the Black Death should have been inflicted upon the Scots by the English, given that the Anglo-Scottish conflict dominated political concerns throughout the fourteenth century and beyond. The 'foul death of the English' summarises well the contemporary Scottish understanding of the Black Death.

CONCLUSION

Our discussion of the Black Death in Scotland comes full circle here. In noting the apparently odd name that contemporaries attributed to the epidemic of the mid-fourteenth century, we are struck by the parallels it presents with John of Fordun's contemporary account which described the loathsome way in which so many people were killed. However, as part one of this book discussed, in terms of mortality the impact of the Black Death in Scotland was probably less severe than elsewhere. The clinical nature of the disease is of importance in ascertaining this. Contrary to the traditional assumption that the Black Death was what we would now identify as bubonic plague, it is likely that something else was responsible, either on its own or, more probably, in combination with several other diseases. Bubonic plague is spread by the fleas of infected rodents that feed on humans if their preferred host – the brown, or perhaps black, rat – is not available. Archaeological evidence has been unable to prove conclusively that rats existed in Scotland at the time of the Black Death. In any case, recent research has strongly indicated that the pandemic of the mid-fourteenth century spread too quickly and unhindered to be attributable to a rodent-borne infection. Removing the importance of rats as vectors of transmission negates the debate that has influenced much scholarly work on the effects of the plague, namely that conditions in Scotland were too cold to allow rats and their fleas to survive. It is far more likely that the epidemic which broke out in Scotland in 1349 was actually a viral disease transmitted directly from person to person. This may have included an element of pneumonic plague, as contemporary accounts describe how victims died within a matter of days, perhaps even within twenty-four hours. This strain of plague is almost invariably fatal and spreads from person to person remarkably quickly, especially in cold conditions. Its ability to spread most effectively (and thereby kill virulently) is determined by a dense population distribution, with humans living in close proximity and in a dense pattern of inhabitation over a wide area. In the mid-fourteenth century Scotland's population was sparse and its uneven distribution dictated by mountainous, rugged terrain that concentrated the majority of inhabitants north and east of the central belt.

Most of them lived in scattered rural communities that maintained essential contact with urban centres, wherein conditions were equally rife to allow interpersonal transmission. It is probable, therefore, that the Black Death in Scotland was a viral disease that quickly killed many people in close proximity, but whose impact was limited in its geographical spread by the speed with which victims died.

Contemporary accounts support this, both in the descriptions of symptoms and in the limited effects the Black Death apparently had. The reticence of Scottish chroniclers stands in sharp contrast to the majority of commentators who detail the horrors of the epidemic as well as the devastation it caused. While John of Fordun noted the fear and repulsion plague caused, his estimation that 'nearly a third' of the population died is remarkably low, especially given chroniclers' tendency to exaggerate. Furthermore, he made no comment on the subsequent effects of the epidemic that were lamented in such detail by contemporaries elsewhere. We must look to other sources to ascertain the likely impact of the Black Death. As part two of this book showed, Scotland followed the European pattern of economic fortunes in the wake of the epidemic: the price of staple goods fell, whilst the disposable income available to those who survived plague meant that demand for luxury goods temporarily increased and was sustained almost until the end of the fourteenth century. The economic boom in the immediate aftermath of plague was thereafter reversed and Europe entered a period of protracted commercial decline. For peasants the Black Death ushered in a temporary period of prosperity and increased social mobility, as the labour shortage meant they were able to demand higher wages and lower rents. The corollary of this was a downturn in fortunes for landlords, many of whom were forced to relinquish their lands and concentrate on the less labour-intensive pastoral farming. While these trends were evidenced in Scotland, it is unlikely that they were felt to the same extent as elsewhere, probably because the mortality from the Black Death was comparatively lower. Unlike England and France, there were no perceptible class tensions, many landowners continued to invest lavishly in residences and other cultural pursuits and the Crown's fortunes followed those of the national economy as they derived largely from customs revenues. The balance of royal finances was generally stable, therefore, as the expenditure necessitated in paying David II's ransom was offset by the revenue which could be commanded from booming exports, until the downturn at the end of the century. The Church's fortunes fluctuated in a similarly complementary manner, as the decline in the value of its lands was temporarily compensated for by the booming wool market. The clergy was perhaps one of the hardest-hit groups within society in terms of mortality but the effects this had elsewhere – an increase in pluralism and the appointment of unqualified incumbents – were apparently no worse in Scotland than they had been before the mid-fourteenth century.

Even if the Black Death did not have a particularly disastrous effect on Scotland in quantitative terms, the psychological impact on society of the death of 'even' a quarter of the population must have been devastating. In gauging the extent of this, the human response is perhaps the most telling but it is also the aspect for which the least evidence survives. For contemporaries the instinctive reaction to plague and its victims was probably one of the worst aspects of the Black Death. Although the chroniclers are generally reticent, Fordun's assertion that people were too scared of becoming infected even to visit dying loved ones, is strikingly similar to Boccaccio's comment that in Florence:

> divers apprehensions and imaginations were engendered in the minds of such as were left alive; inclining almost all of them to the same harsh resolution; to wit, to shun and abhor all contact with the sick and all that belonged to them, thinking thereby to make each his own health secure.

Crosses on clothes: victims of plague (and other such diseases) were often forcibly identified by distinctive markings such as crosses on their clothes or being made to carry a white stick. This was undertaken in order to warn the public so that they could avoid contact with infection. It also ensured the sufferer's ostracism

The horrible ways in which plague was manifested (such as vomiting blood and displaying stinking, fetid sores) were no doubt exacerbated by the knowledge in the medieval mind of plague's ultimate origins. As part three of this book discussed, the Bible presented contemporaries with a clear interpretive framework for the spiritual (though not clinical) cause of pestilence. As integral members of the international Catholic Church, fourteenth-century Scots were well aware that plague was divine retribution for the collective sins of society. Upon first hearing about it, they emphatically believed it to be God's vengeance on the English (until it broke out amongst themselves, of course). They were also familiar with the fundamental remedy for the scourge, as it was only by appeasing God through penitent confession that the epidemic would be brought to an end. The fundamental elements of Christian worship – cults of saints, relics and pilgrimages – were almost certainly widely turned to in Scotland when the Black Death broke out. The spiritual interpretation of plague did not preclude belief in secondary causes and learned physicians also looked to scientific explanations to prevent and treat plague. Contemporary clinical understanding of the Black Death was based on the dominant interpretation of all diseases as emanating from a humoural imbalance within the individual, with celestial and terrestrial causes also having a significant influence. Medical knowledge in fourteenth-century Scotland was in line with continental beliefs and, through their university attendance, Scots made a vibrant and important contribution to the European intellectual climate. Evidence exists of both a documentary and archaeological nature to demonstrate the state of medical theory and practice at the time of the Black Death and to indicate the likely medical, bureaucratic and spiritual responses to plague.

What might we conclude about the impact of the Black Death in Scotland? In many ways the course of, effects of, and responses to, fourteenth-century plague were remarkably similar to elsewhere in Europe. However, it is perhaps equally telling that other reactions were markedly different or altogether absent. We may remind ourselves of Philip Ziegler's belief that Scotland escaped with 'so light a scar' from plague and of Alexander Grant's judgement that the Black Death was 'the worst disaster suffered by the people of Scotland in recorded history.' Our conclusion must be that in every sense these apparently opposing pronouncements on Scotland's experience of the Black Death are both absolutely correct. In quantitative terms Scotland was not so greatly affected by the epidemic, with the loss of perhaps 'only' a quarter of the population. But in qualitative terms – which, after all, would have mattered more to contemporaries – inhabitants of fourteenth-century Scotland were as deeply and as pervasively affected by the Black Death as their counterparts throughout the rest of the known world.

BIBLIOGRAPHY

LIST OF ILLUSTRATIONS

INDEX

BIBLIOGRAPHY

[Anon.], *An Account of the Chapel of Roslin* (Edinburgh, 1778).

Anderson, J., A *History of Edinburgh from the Earliest Period to the Completion of the Half Century 1850* (Edinburgh, 1856).

Appleby, A., 'Epidemics and Famine in the Little Ice Age', *Journal of Interdisciplinary History* 10, (1980).

Aries, P., *The Hour of Our Death* (London, 1983).

Arrizabalaga, Jon, 'Facing the Black Death: Perceptions and Reactions of University Medical Practitioners', in Garcia-Ballester, L., French, R., Arrizabalaga, J., and Cunningham, A. (eds), *Practical Medicine from Salerno to the Black Death* (Cambridge, 1994).

Aston, M., 'Death', in Horrox, R.,(ed.), *Fifteenth Century Attitudes: Perceptions of Society in Late Medieval England* (Cambridge, 1994).

Bannerman, J., *The Beatons: a Medical Kindred in the Classical Gaelic Tradition* (Edinburgh, 1986).

Barron, C.M., and Harper-Bill, C. (eds), *The Church in Pre-Reformation Society: Essays in Honour of F.R.H. DuBoulay* (Suffolk, 1985).

Benedictow, O.J., *The Black Death, 1346-1353: the Complete History* (Woodbridge, 2004).

Benedictow, O.J., *Plague in the Late Medieval Nordic Countries: Epidemiological Studies* (Oslo, 1992).

Biraben, J.N., *Les Hommes et la Peste en France et dans les Pays Européens et Méditerranéens*, 2 vols (Paris, 1975-76).

Blockmans, W.P., 'The Social and Economic Effects of Plague in the

Low Countries, 1349-1500', *Revue Belge de Philologie et d'Histoire* 58 (1980).

Boase, T.S.R., *Death in the Middle Ages: Mortality, Judgement and Remembrance* (London, 1972).

Boccaccio, G., *The Decameron* (New York, 1982).

Bowsky, W., 'The Impact of the Black Death upon Sienese Government and Society', *Speculum* 39, (1964).

Bradley, L., 'Some Medical Aspects of Plague', in *Local Population Studies, The Plague Reconsidered: a New Look at its Origins and Effects in 16th and 17th Century England* (Matlock, 1977).

Brodman, J.W., *Charity and Welfare: Hospitals and the Poor in Medieval Catalonia* (Philadelphia, 1998).

Brody, S.N., *The Disease of the Soul: Leprosy in Medieval Literature*, (Ithaca, 1974).

Carlin, M., 'Medieval English Hospitals', in Granshaw, L., and Porter, R. (eds), *The Hospital in History* (London, 1989).

Carmichael, A., *Epidemic Diseases in Early Renaissance Florence* (Ann Arbor, 1980).

Carpentier, E., *Une Ville Devant la Peste: Orvieto et la Peste Noire de 1348* (Paris, 1962).

Chambers, W. (ed.), *Charters and Documents Relating to the Burgh of Peebles, with Extracts from the Records of the Burgh, 1165-1710* (Edinburgh, 1872).

Cipolla, C.M., *Miasmas and Disease: Public Health and the Environment in the Pre-Industrial Age* (New Haven, 1992).

Clark, J.M., *The Dance of Death in the Middle Ages and the Renaissance* (Glasgow, 1950).

Cohen, J., *The Friars and the Jews: the Evolution of Medieval Anti-Judaism* (Ithaca, 1982).

Cohn, S., 'Criminality and the State in Renaissance Florence, 1344-1466', *Journal of Social History* 14 (1980).

Collino, M., *The Dance of Death in Book Illustration* (Columbia, Missouri, 1978).

Comrie, J.D., *History of Scottish Medicine*, vol. 1 (London, 1932).

Conrad, L., 'Epidemic Disease in Formal and Popular Thought in Early Islamic Society', in Ranger, T., and Slack, P. (eds), *Epidemics and Ideas: Essays on the Historical Perception of Pestilence* (Cambridge, 1992).

Cook, W.B. (ed.), *The Stirling Antiquary* (Stirling, 1904).

Cranna, J., *History of Fraserburgh*, (Aberdeen, 1914).

Crawfurd, R., *Plague and Pestilence in Literature and Art* (Oxford, 1914).

Creighton, C., *A History of Epidemics in Britain* (Cambridge, 1891).

Croft Dickinson, W., 'Burgh Life from Burgh Records', *Aberdeen University Review* 33 (1946).

Croft Dickinson, W. (ed.), *Early Records of the Burgh of Aberdeen, 1317, 1398-1407* (Edinburgh, 1957).

Cunningham, A., 'Transforming Plague: the Laboratory and the Identity of Infectious Disease', in Cunningham, A. and Williams, P. (eds), *The Laboratory Revolution in Medicine* (Cambridge, 1992).

Dalyell, J.G., *The Darker Superstitions of Scotland, Illustrated from History and Practice* (Edinburgh, 1884).

Davidson, J., *Inverurie and the Earldom of the Garioch* (Edinburgh, 1878).

Davies, R.A., 'The Effect of the Black Death on the Parish Priests of the Medieval Diocese of Coventry and Lichfield', *Historical Research* 62 (1989).

Ditchburn, D., 'Trade with Northern Europe, 1297-1540', in Lynch,

Michael, Spearman, Michael, and Stell, Geoffrey (eds), *The Scottish Medieval Town* (Edinburgh, 1988).

Ditchburn, D., *Scotland and Europe: the Medieval Kingdom and its Contacts with Christendom, 1214-1560* (East Linton, 2000).

Dohar, W.J., *The Black Death and Pastoral Leadership: The Diocese of Hereford in the Fourteenth Century* (Philadelphia, 1995).

Dols, M., 'The Comparative Communal Responses to the Black Death in Muslim and Christian Societies', *Viator*, 5 (1974).

Dols, M., *The Black Death in the Middle East* (Princeton, 1977).

Dols, M., 'The Second Plague Pandemic and its Recurrence in the Middle East: 1347-1894', *Journal of the Economic and Social History of the Orient* 22 (1979).

Ell, S.R., 'Interhuman Transmission of Medieval Plague', *Bulletin of the History of Medicine* 54 (1980).

Ewan, E., 'The Age of Bon-Accord: Aberdeen in the Fourteenth Century', in Smith, J.S. (ed.), *New Light on Medieval Aberdeen* (Aberdeen, 1985).

Fischer, T.A., *The Scots in Germany* (Edinburgh, 1902).

Fischer, T.A., *The Scots in Eastern and Western Prussia* (Edinburgh, 1903).

Fitch, A.B., 'Assumptions about Plague in Late Medieval Scotland', *Scotia* 11 (1987).

Foege, W.H., 'Plagues: Perceptions of Risk and Social Responses', in Mack, Arien (ed.), *In Time of Plague: the History and Social Consequences of Lethal Epidemic Disease* (New York, 1991).

Fraser, D., *Montrose (Before 1700)* (Montrose, 1967).

French, R., Arrizabalaga, J., Cunningham, A., and García-Ballester, L. (eds), *Medicine from the Black Death to the French Disease* (Aldershot, 1998).

Gottfried, R., *The Black Death: Natural and Human Disaster in Medieval Europe* (New York, 1983).

Gottfried, R., 'English Medical Practitioners, 1340-1530', *Bulletin of Medical History* 58 (1984).

Grant, A., *Independence and Nationhood: Scotland 1306-1469* (London, 1984).

Hamilton, D., *The Healers: a History of Medicine in Scotland* (Edinburgh, 1981).

Hatcher, J., *Plague, Population and the English Economy, 1348-1530* (London, 1977).

Hatcher, J., 'England in the Aftermath of the Black Death', *Past and Present* 144 (1994).

Henderson, J., 'The Parish and the Poor in Florence at the Time of the Black Death: the Case of S. Frediano', *Continuity and Change* 3 (1988).

Henderson, J., 'Epidemics in Renaissance Florence: Medical Theory and Government Response', in Bulst, N., and Delort, R. (eds), *Maladie et Société (XIIe-XVIIIe Siècles)* (Paris, 1989).

Herlihy, D., *The Black Death and the Transformation of the West* (Harvard, 1977).

Horrox, R. (ed.), *The Black Death* (Manchester, 1994).

Huizinga, J., *The Waning of the Middle Ages* (London, 1924).

Hume Brown, P. (ed.), *Early Travellers in Scotland* (Edinburgh, 1891).

Hume Brown, P. (ed.), *Scotland Before 1700 from Contemporary Documents* (Edinburgh, 1893).

Huppert, G., *After the Black Death* (Bloomington, 1986).

Jackson, G., and Lythe, S.G.E. (eds), *The Port of Montrose: a History of its Harbour, Trade and Shipping* (Tayport, 1993).

Jacquart, D., and Thomasset, C., *Sexuality and Medicine in the Middle Ages* (Cambridge, 1988).

Karlen, A., *Plague's Progress: A Social History of Man and Disease* (London, 1996).

Karlsson, Gunnar, 'Plague Without Rats: the Case of Fifteenth Century Iceland', *Journal of Medieval History* 22 (1996).

Keith, A., *A Thousand Years of Aberdeen* (Aberdeen, 1972).

Kelly, J., *The Great Mortality: an Intimate History of the Black Death* (London, 2006).

Kelly, M., *A History of the Black Death in Ireland* (Stroud, 2001).

Kennedy, W., *Annals of Aberdeen, from the Reign of King William the Lion, to the End of the Year 1818*, 2 vols (London, 1818).

Kinsley, J. (ed.), *The Poems of William Dunbar* (Oxford, 1979).

Lachmund, J., and Stollberg, G. (eds), *The Social Construction of Illness: Illness and Medical Knowledge in Past and Present* (Stuttgart, 1992).

Langholf, V., *Medical Theories in Hippocrates* (Berlin, 1990).

Lerner, Robert, 'The Black Death and Western European Eschatological Mentalities', *American Historical Review* 86 (1981).

Love, D., *Scottish Kirkyards* (London, 1989).

Lynch, M., *Scotland: a New History* (London, 1991).

McNeill, P.G.B., and MacQueen, H.L. (eds), *Atlas of Scottish History to 1707* (Edinburgh, 1996).

McNeill, W., *Plagues and Peoples* (Oxford, 1977).

McPherson, J.M., *Primitive Beliefs in the North-East of Scotland* (London, 1929).

McVaugh, M., *Medicine Before the Plague: Practitioners and their Patients in the Crown of Aragon, 1285-1345* (Cambridge, 1993).

Maxwell, A., *The History of Old Dundee* (Edinburgh, 1884).

Maxwell, A., *Old Dundee, Ecclesiastical, Burghal, and Social, Prior to the Reformation* (Edinburgh, 1891).

Mayhew, N., 'Alexander III – A Silver Age? An Essay in Scottish

Medieval Economic History', in Reid, N. (ed.), *Scotland in the Reign of Alexander III, 1249-1286* (Edinburgh, 1990).

Mayhew, N., and Gemmill, E., *Changing Values in Medieval Scotland: a Study of Prices, Money, and Weights and Measures* (Cambridge, 1995).

Moore, R.I., *The Formation of a Persecuting Society: Power and Deviance in Western Europe, 950-1250* (Oxford, 1987)

Moran, J., 'Clerical Recruitment in the Diocese of York, 1340-1530: Data and Commentary', *Journal of Ecclesiastical History* 34 (1983).

Morrison, I., 'Climatic Changes and Human Geography: Scotland in a North Atlantic Context', *Northern Studies* 27 (1990).

Mowat, S., *The Port of Leith: its History and its People* (Edinburgh, 1993).

Mullett, C.F., 'Plague Policy in Scotland, 16th-17th Centuries', *Osiris* 9 (1950).

Murray, J.C. (ed.), *Excavations in the Medieval Burgh of Aberdeen, 1973-81* (Edinburgh, 1982).

Naphy, W., and Spicer, A., *The Black Death and the History of Plagues, 1345-1730* (Stroud, 2000).

Nikiforuk, A., *The Fourth Horseman: A Short History of Epidemics, Plagues and other Scourges* (London, 1993).

Nutton, V., 'Continuity or Rediscovery? The City Physician in Classical Antiquity and Medieval Italy', in Russell, A. (ed.), *The Town and State Physician from the Middle Ages to the Enlightenment* (Wolfenbüttel, 1981).

Nutton, V., 'The Seeds of Disease: an Explanation of Contagion and Infection from the Greeks to the Renaissance', *Medical History* 27 (1983).

O'Malley, C.D. (ed.), *The History of Medical Education* (Berkley, 1970).

Ormrod, W.M., and Lindley, P.G. (eds), *The Black Death in England*

(Stamford, 1996).

Palmer, R., 'The Church, Leprosy, and Plague in Medieval and Early Modern Europe', in Sheils, W.J. (ed.), *The Church and Healing, Studies in Church History* 19 (Oxford, 1982).

Peacock, D., *Perth: its Annals and its Archives* (Perth, 1849).

Platt, C., *King Death: the Black Death and its Aftermath in Late Medieval England* (London, 1996).

Pollitzer, R., *Plague* (Geneva, 1954).

Pullan, B., 'Support and Redeem: Charity and Poor Relief in Italian Cities from the Fourteenth to the Seventeenth Century', *Continuity and Change* 3 (1988).

Rawcliffe, C., *Medicine and Society in Later Medieval England* (Stroud, 1995).

Renwick, R., and Lindsay, J., *History of Glasgow*, vol. 1 (Glasgow, 1921).

Richards, P., *The Medieval Leper and His Northern Heirs* (Cambridge, 1977).

Roberts, A., 'The Plague in England', *History Today* 30 (1980).

Robertson, J., *The Book of Bon-Accord: a Guide to the City of Aberdeen* (Aberdeen, 1839).

Ross, A., *An Account of the Antiquity of the City of Aberdeen with the Price of Grain and Cattle, from the Year 1435 to 1591* (Aberdeen, ?1780).

Ross, I., 'Dunbar's "Vision of the Four Last Things", in Aitken, A.J., McDiarmid, M.P., and Thomson, D.S. (eds), *Bards and Makars* (Glasgow, 1977).

Russell, A. (ed.), *The Town and State Physician from the Middle Ages to the Enlightenment* (Wolfenbüttel, 1981).

Sabine, E.L., 'Butchering in Mediaeval London', *Speculum* 8 (1933).

Sabine, E.L., 'Latrines and Cesspools of Mediaeval London', *Speculum* 9 (1934).

Sabine, E.L., 'City Cleaning in Mediaeval London', *Speculum* 12 (1937).

Scott, S. and Duncan, C., *Return of the Black Death: the World's Greatest Serial Killer* (London, 2005)

Shatzmiller, J., Jews, *Medicine and Medieval Society* (Berkeley, 1994).

Shrewsbury, J.F.D., *A History of Bubonic Plague in the British Isles* (Cambridge, 1970).

Simpson, G.G. (ed.), *Scotland and Scandinavia, 800-1800* (Edinburgh, 1990).

Simpson, G.G. (ed.), *Scotland and the Low Countries, 1124-1994* (East Linton, 1996).

Siraisi, N., *Medieval and Early Renaissance Medicine: an Introduction to Knowledge and Practice* (Chicago, 1990).

Skene, W.F. (ed.), *John of Fordun's Chronicle of the Scottish Nation* (Edinburgh, 1993).

Smail, D.L., 'Accommodating Plague in Medieval Marseille', *Continuity and Change* 11 (1996).

Smout, T.C., 'Coping with Plague in Sixteenth and Seventeenth Century Scotland', *Scotia* 2 (1978).

Stones, J.A. (ed.), *Three Scottish Carmelite Friaries: Excavations at Aberdeen, Linlithgow and Perth, 1980-1986* (Edinburgh, 1989).

Thom, W., *The History of Aberdeen, Containing an Account of the Rise, Progress and Extension of the City from a Remote Period to the Present Day*, 2 vols (Aberdeen, 1811).

Thorndike, L., 'Sanitation, Baths, and Street-Cleaning in the Middle Ages and Renaissance', *Speculum* 3 (1928).

Thrupp, S.L., 'Social Control in the Medieval Town', *Journal of Economic History* 1 (1941).

Torrie, E.P.D., 'Medieval Dundee: a Town and its People', *Abertay Historical Society Publications* 30 (1990).

Torrie, E.P.D., 'The Early Urban Site of New Aberdeen: a Reappraisal of the Evidence', *Northern Scotland* 12 (1992).

Watt, D.E.R., *Biographical Dictionary of Scottish Graduates to AD 1410* (Oxford, 1977).

Watt, D.E.R., 'Scottish University Men of the Thirteenth and Fourteenth Centuries', in T.C. Smout (ed.), *Scotland and Europe, 1200-1850* (Edinburgh, 1986).

Watt, W., *The County Histories of Scotland: Aberdeen and Banff* (Edinburgh, 1900).

Waugh, S.L., *England in the Reign of Edward III* (Cambridge, 1991).

Whyte, I.D., *Scotland Before the Industrial Revolution: An Economic and Social History, c.1050-c.1750* (London, 1995).

Wigley, T., Ingram, M., and Farmer, G. (eds), *Climate and History: Studies in Past Climates and Their Impact on Man* (Cambridge, 1981).

Williman, D. (ed.), *The Black Death: the Impact of the Fourteenth-Century Plague* (Binghamton, 1982).

Willsher, B., *Understanding Scottish Graveyards* (Edinburgh, 1995).

Wilson, R., *An Historical Account and Delineation of Aberdeen* (Aberdeen, 1822).

Wood, H.H. (ed.), *The Poems and Fables of Robert Henryson* (Edinburgh, 1958).

Wood, J.M., 'Some Account of the Plague in Edinburgh in Olden Days', *Caledonian Medical Journal* 11 (1918).

Wright, J. (ed.), *Parish, Church and People: Local Studies in Lay Religion, 1350-1750* (London, 1988).

Yeoman, P., *Medieval Scotland: an Archaeological Perspective* (London, 1995).

Ziegler, P., *The Black Death* (New York, 1969).

LIST OF ILLUSTRATIONS

INDEX

TEMPUS REVEALING HISTORY

Scotland
From Prehistory to the Present
FIONA WATSON
The Scotsman **Bestseller**
£9.99
0 7524 2591 9

1314 Bannockburn
ARYEH NUSBACHER
'Written with good-humoured verve as
befits a rattling "yarn of sex, violence and
terror"'
History Scotland
£9.99
0 7524 2982 5

Flodden
NIALL BARR
'Tells the story brilliantly'
The Sunday Post
£9.99
0 7524 2593 5

Scotland's Black Death
The Foul Death of the English
KAREN JILLINGS
'So incongruously enjoyable a read, and so
attractively presented by the publishers'
The Scotsman
£12.99
978 07524 3732 3

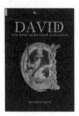

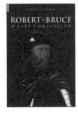

David I The King Who Made Scotland
RICHARD ORAM
'Enthralling... sets just the right tone as the
launch-volume of an important new series
of royal biographies' *Magnus Magnusson*
£17.99
0 7524 2825 X

The Kings & Queens of Scotland
RICHARD ORAM
'A serious, readable work that sweeps across
a vast historical landscape' *The Daily Mail*
£12.99
0 7524 3814 X

The Second Scottish Wars of Independence 1332–1363
CHRIS BROWN
'Explodes the myth of the invincible Bruces...
lucid and highly readable' *History Scotland*
£12.99
0 7524 3812 3

Robert the Bruce: A Life Chronicled
CHRIS BROWN
'A masterpiece of research'
The Scots Magazine
£30
0 7524 2575 7

If you are interested in purchasing other books published by Tempus, or in case you have difficulty finding any Tempus
books in your local bookshop, you can also place orders directly through our website

www.tempus-publishing.com